BRITAIN'S WILDLIFE
RARITIES AND INTRODUCTIONS

BRITAIN'S WILDLIFE
RARITIES AND INTRODUCTIONS

BY RICHARD FITTER

WITH 35 PAINTINGS BY
JOHN LEIGH-PEMBERTON

FOREWORD BY
H.R.H. THE DUKE OF EDINBURGH, K.G., K.T.
(President of the World Wildlife Fund, British National Appeal)

PREFACE BY
PETER SCOTT, C.B.E., D.S.C.

published by
NICHOLAS KAYE LTD
in association with
MIDLAND BANK LTD

First published by
NICHOLAS KAYE LTD
194–200 Bishopsgate, London E.C.2
1966

Printed in England by
ADLARD AND SON LTD
LONDON AND DORKING

The days when wild birds and animals existed in spite of mankind are long since past.

To-day any living creature which exists in the wild does so only with our sanction. That is why it is so important that we should try to understand the circumstances which make some creatures rare and others plentiful.

Mankind in the past has been responsible, wittingly or unwittingly, for the extermination of a great many species. From now on we should see to it that no species becomes endangered by our ignorance or neglect.

This series of books should do much to make people aware of the difficulties and dangers which Britain's wild life has to face in this modern world.

1966.

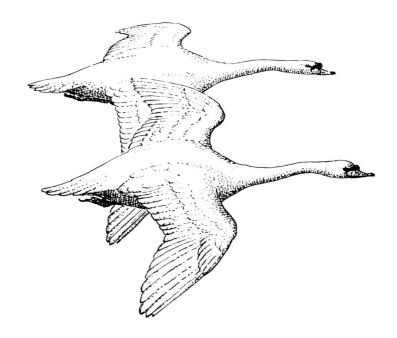

Preface
by
Peter Scott, C.B.E., D.S.C.
Chairman of the World Wildlife Fund
(British National Appeal)

As Chairman of the World Wildlife Fund, I have a special interest in the rare animals; and the Fund is as much concerned about the birds and beasts of Britain—the natural communities of wildlife—as it is with the creatures threatened with extinction in far away places. I am also interested in introduced animals, because of the effects they have had on the native wildlife and on the natural scene.

The Wildfowl Trust has been largely responsible for adding one new bird to the British List—the North American Ruddy Duck—as mentioned on page 22, and I doubt if it will have any effect save to provide one more attractive bird for the enjoyment of bird-watchers.

Reintroduction is one of the techniques supported by the World Wildlife Fund in its effort to save rare animals all over the world. The Fund has, for instance, supported The Wildfowl Trust's reintroduction of the Nene or Hawaiian Goose to the Hawaiian Island of Maui, and the introduction of the White Rhinoceros to the Murchison Falls National Park in Uganda. It has also joined with The Fauna Preservation Society and The Zoological Society of London in establishing the World of Arabian Oryx at Phoenix, Arizona.

The subject matter of this book is therefore very germane to my current efforts to save the world's wildlife through the medium of The World Wildlife Fund, the Survival Service Commission of the International Union for the Conservation of Nature, and the Fauna Preservation Society, in all three of which I am happy to be associated with the author, who is the Honorary Secretary of the Fauna Preservation Society, a member of the Survival Service Commission, and a member of the Allocations Committee of the British National Appeal of the World Wildlife Fund.

Richard Fitter is also well known as a writer and broadcaster on wildlife subjects, being Open-air Correspondent of *The Observer,* and author of standard field guides to birds, their nests and eggs, bird-watching and wild flowers, as well as of the only book so far published on the introduced animals of the British Isles, *The Ark in Our Midst.* He was therefore an obvious choice to write the text when Midland Bank, who deserve all praise for their use of wildlife themes in their advertising, decided to support the publishers in their plan to issue in book form the two series of admirable paintings by John Leigh-Pemberton on British Wildlife, Rarities and Introductions.

Slimbridge
June 1966

Contents

Introduction

Fifty-two of the animals illustrated in this book are either rare, scarce or at least local, the remaining twenty-six being introduced aliens, some of which also happen to be rare or uncommon. The total of seventy-eight is composed of fourteen mammals, fifty-two birds, six fishes and six butterflies.

Some animals have probably always been rare in the British Isles, others have only become rare during the past two hundred years, while yet others that were once rare are gradually, or even, as in the case of the collared dove, rapidly becoming commoner. Rarity and scarcity are, however, imprecise terms that cover many different conditions of a stock or population of animals. Although the short answer to the question why so many animals have become rare, and some even extinct, such as the sea eagle, is simply that there are too many people in most parts of Britain south of the Highland line, natural factors still play a substantial part in determining the status of most animals. Indeed for the great majority of invertebrate animals climatic and other natural factors are still predominant. But the larger an animal is, the more it is likely to find its way of life conflicting with that of man.

The most important of these natural factors making for rarity or abundance in an animal are the climate and its habitat, including food supply. We still know extremely little about the effects of climate on animal populations, but it is safe to say that our cool summers are more important in this respect than our damp winters, although if the present series of hard winters continues the situation may change. A long-term climatic change, bringing cooler summers, is believed to underlie the recent decline of the wryneck to the status of one of our rarest breeding birds. The red-backed shrike is afflicted in much the same way, and may have to be classified as rare within the next ten years. Nobody knows just how the cooler summers have affected these two birds, but the presumption is that certain insects on which they depend for food have become rarer. On the other hand, the recent hard winters, combined with the steady erosion of its heathland habitat, have made the Dartford warbler a very rare bird. Other birds much affected by the winters of 1961–2 and 1962–3 are the stonechat, goldcrest and green woodpecker, which though not in any real sense rare are still in 1966 much scarcer than they were five or six years ago.

Natural factors affecting the habitat are much easier to understand, but also begin to impinge on the artificial factors, for destruction of habitat is the major human cause of rarity among animals. However, some habitat factors are still purely natural, such as the large territory needed by the golden eagle to feed itself, so that eagles are inevitably widely spread and so less common than a smaller bird of prey, such as the kestrel. A special case of rarity due to the restriction of habitat is presented by animals confined to small islands, as with the Scilly shrew and the Orkney vole. But sometimes animals on the edge of their range make artificial islands for themselves, by not spreading into areas which to the human eye look identical, but evidently possess some subtle natural difference that escapes us. Good examples of this are the limited range of the Lulworth skipper butterfly along the south coast of England, of the introduced edible dormouse in the Chilterns, and of the crested tit in the Spey valley.

Turning now to the human factors that make animals rare, or in the last resort even extinct, it is inevitable in modern conditions that an expanding human population of the British Isles, in providing themselves with living space, food and other amenities, should interfere to some extent with the living space, food supply and other amenities of the wild animal and plant populations. This does not, of course, mean that the process of interference should be allowed to proceed unchecked, but it does mean that we cannot hope to preserve unscathed every acre of what is at present open countryside. Careful planning is needed to ensure that those areas which are richest in wildlife are preserved for posterity.

There is no doubt that the prime cause of the rarity of the native, as distinct from introduced animals in this book is destruction of the habitat. Certain habitats, such as marshland and fens, with their bitterns, marsh harriers and swallow-tail butterflies, and heathland, with its hobbies, Montagu's harriers and Dartford warblers, are especially vulnerable. On the other hand, we must not lose sight of the fact that the destruction of one habitat usually means the creation of another. A drained marsh may mean fewer water rails and reed warblers, but the resulting farmland will house more skylarks and partridges. What is necessary is to ensure that not all marshland and fens are drained, so that adequate stocks of the marshland birds and other animals are enabled to survive.

The next most important human cause of rarity among animals is direct killing by man. This applies especially to many of our rarer birds and beasts of prey, such as the pine marten, polecat, kite, osprey and sea eagle, the last-named having been actually exterminated as a breeding species. Most of these have been persecuted down the ages by gamekeepers in the supposed interests of game preservation. Modern research on grouse populations by Dr David Jenkins and his co-workers in Aberdeenshire shows how futile this traditional killing of predators has been, but this will not give us back our lost birds of prey. In a few instances, such as the osprey and sea eagle threatened by game preservers and the large copper butterfly threatened by drainage of its habitat, the actual *coup de grâce* has been administered by kleptomaniac collectors of eggs and skins, one of whom did his best to prevent the re-establishment of the osprey as a British breeding species.

Sometimes the killing by man is an indirect and unintended side effect of some quite different activity, such as the widespread use of organochlorine pesticides, which has made the peregrine falcon a rare bird and has made almost all our other birds of prey less common than they were ten years ago. These pesticides are persistent, and their residues collect in the birds' prey and so build up in excessive quantities in their own bodies. Fortunately action seems to have been taken in time, for the latest information about the peregrine suggests that its slide towards extinction may have been halted.

Only two breeding birds have actually become extinct in the British Isles in this century, the osprey and the sea eagle. Now the osprey has come back, as have four marshland birds that became extinct in the last century, the avocet, marsh harrier, bittern and black-tailed godwit. We still await the announcement of the return of other losses of the last century, such as the ruff, the black tern and Savi's warbler.

So far only breeding species have been mentioned, but there is another quite distinct form of rarity, the occasional visitor or vagrant. Here human intervention has little or nothing to do with the rarity. It is even doubtful if the reprehensible Victorian habit of shooting any strange bird on sight had the effect of making it rarer or preventing it from becoming commoner. These birds are either just overshooting their normal breeding range, as with the hoopoe, roller or bee-eater, or straying a little off the course of their normal migration, as with the black tern, bluethroat or grey-headed wagtail, or are completely lost wanderers, such as the blue-cheeked bee-eater. A few rarities, especially the waxwing and crossbill among birds, and the Bath white and Queen of Spain fritillary among butterflies, are irregular wanderers which represent an overspill from an unusually abundant population elsewhere.

Rarity is a quality of perennial appeal, by no means confined to the natural world, and whatever the causes of their scarcity, lovers of Britain's countryside and wildlife naturally cherish the rarer creatures more than the commoner ones, and join together for concerted action to protect them. Until the Council for Nature was founded in 1958, however, there was no central body with an interest in preserving the whole field of wildlife in Britain, and now the Council, which is primarily a co-ordinating body, has been buttressed by the setting up, as a purely fund-raising body, of the British National Appeal of the World Wildlife Fund in 1961. The more specialized organizations already working in the field include, in the order of their foundation, the Royal Society for the Protection of Birds (1889); the Fauna Preservation Society (1903), which is mainly concerned with wildlife overseas but also includes within its ambit British land verte-brates other than birds; the Society for the Promotion of Nature Reserves (1912), which acts as the umbrella body for the County Naturalists' Trusts (1926–64); the British Section of the International Council for Bird Preservation (1922); and the Wildfowl Trust (1946), a body which is interested in the conservation of ducks, geese and swans throughout the world. The Royal Entomological Society of London (1833) and the Botanical Society of the British Isles (1836) both have special committees concerned with the conservation of insects and plants respectively, which maintain close liaison with the Nature Conservancy (1949) the official body responsible, under the National Environment Research Council (1965) for the conservation of wildlife in

Great Britain. The addresses of all these bodies will be found on page 94.

The introduced animals present quite a different set of problems, although many of them, such as the edible dormouse, the Chinese water deer and Reeves's pheasant, are also either local or rare. There are two major reasons why animals have been deliberately introduced into the British Isles: for sporting purposes, to augment diminishing game stocks, as with the sika deer, pheasant and red-legged partridge; and for amenity or aesthetic reasons, to embellish parks and private pleasure grounds, whence they have often escaped. Examples of the latter group are the muntjac or barking deer, grey squirrel and Canada goose. A third reason, scientific experiment, applies in comparatively few cases, such as the reintroduction of the large copper butterfly, and the introduction of the common frog into Ireland nearly three hundred years ago.

It is always a puzzle why just a few of the numerous attempts to introduce alien animals into the British countryside should succeed apparently haphazardly, while the vast majority fail. It took forty years, for instance, to establish the little owl, which now seems so much a part of the landscape. On the other hand, all the marsh frogs in Romney Marsh and adjacent parts of Kent and Sussex stem from a dozen released in a single garden pond just over thirty years ago. Probably many attempts have been made with too few individuals, and often insufficient care has been taken to study the habitat and release the animals in the most suitable places.

Experience suggests that the greatest care should be exercised in liberating strange animals anywhere. Some of our most serious pests, such as rats, rabbits, grey squirrels, muskrats, coypus and mink are or were established aliens. It took an expensive official campaign in the 1930s to extirpate the muskrat, which was threatening to undermine our river banks. Fortunately the Minister of Agriculture has now made orders under the Destructive Imported Animals Act, 1932, controlling the import and keeping of muskrats, grey squirrels, mink, coypus and non-indigenous rabbits.

Map of all
the places
mentioned
specifically
in the text

Leslie S. Haywood

Fallow Deer : Carolina Duck

Is the FALLOW DEER a genuinely native British animal? Of the six kinds of deer that run wild in the woods of Britain today, only two are undoubtedly native, the red and the roe, while three more, discussed on pp. 18, 22 and 24, are certainly introduced. A question mark hangs over the fallow deer, which today is not found genuinely wild nearer than southern Europe. A small population might possibly have survived somewhere in the south right through from the genial climate that prevailed around 7000 B.C. to the early eleventh century, when we have the first documentary evidence of their presence. It is perhaps more likely that these Saxon deer descended from some which escaped into the woods in Romano-British days, for we know that the Romans kept fallow deer in Britain. But we may never know where the truth lies.

Today the fallow is our commonest and most widespread deer, and the majority of those now at large in our woods undoubtedly descend from comparatively recent escapes from deer parks. No English county, except perhaps Middlesex, is without its feral fallow deer, and they inhabit also many woodlands of Wales, Scotland and Ireland. Though they may be tiresome to the forester with young plantations or to the farmer with growing crops, the occasional sight of these graceful animals delights most people as they go about the countryside.

Fallow are markedly smaller than red deer, from which they can also be told both by their white-spotted coats, which are brighter in summer, and by the flattened, palmated antlers of the bucks. There are also several herds of a dark, unspotted form, known as black fallow deer. The best known of these has existed for several hundred years in Epping Forest, Essex, where it still numbers about seventy, although many are killed each year by motorists speeding along the main road which runs through the Forest.

The CAROLINA DUCK of North America, where it is also known as wood duck, is almost as handsome as its replendent relative the mandarin (p. 22), but has been much less successful in establishing itself as a breeding species in Britain. Breeding colonies of full-winged Carolinas have existed at various times in the counties of Bedford, Devon, Gloucester, Huntingdon, Northumberland and Surrey, but hardly any of these survive, except for a few at the Wildfowl Trust's collection at Slimbridge on the Severn estuary. Nor has there been any recent news of the colony reported to exist on the Upper Danube at the turn of the century.

As its alternative name suggests, the Carolina duck is a woodland species, nesting in holes in trees and preferring lakes and ponds that are surrounded by woodland. Despite the fact that the ducks of the two species are so hard to tell apart, the Carolina duck will never interbreed with its close relative the mandarin, although it readily does so with mallards and other dabbling ducks.

FALLOW DEER

Family: Deer Family, Cervidae.
Scientific Name: *Dama dama.*
Males are Bucks, *Females* Does and
　Young Fawns.
Length: 5½ feet.
Antlers are cast from February to
　May, and grow again in June and
　July.
Habitat: Woodland.
Breeding Season: Rutting, October–
　November. Fawns born, June–July.
Protection: Close season for Bucks:
　1 May to 31 July. For Does:
　1 March to 31 October in England
　and Wales; 16 February to 20
　October in Scotland.
Further Reading: *Field Guide to
　British Deer; The Ark in Our Midst.*
(See also under *Mammals* on p. 95.)

CAROLINA DUCK

Family: Duck Family, Anatidae.
Scientific Name: *Aix sponsa.*
Males are Drakes, *Females* Ducks and
　Young Ducklings.
Length: 19–20 inches.
Habitat: Neighbourhood of water-
　fowl collections.
Breeding Season: April–May.
Protection: None can be provided
　until the bird becomes an estab-
　lished breeding species in Britain.
Further Reading: *The Waterfowl of
　the World; The Ark in Our Midst.*

17

Sika Deer : Grey Squirrel

The SIKA or JAPANESE DEER is like a small red deer, about the size of a fallow deer and with faint white spots on its summer coat. A native of eastern Asia, it is found in woods in many parts of the British Isles, having either escaped from deer parks or in some districts been deliberately released to provide sport for buckhounds.

Dorset, Argyll (Kintyre), Inverness, Peebles, Kerry and Wicklow are the counties where it is most numerous, and there are smaller numbers in five other English, three other Scottish, and three other Irish counties. The Dorset colony sprang from a few which swam ashore from Brownsea Island in Poole Harbour, where they are now extinct. Those in the New Forest, however, appear to have originated from the Beaulieu estate. The small herd which still survives in the Ribblesdale and Pendle Forest areas on the borders of Lancashire and Yorkshire descends from some turned down sixty years ago for the local buckhounds.

The GREY SQUIRREL provides a classic instance of the folly of introducing an animal into a new country where it may make itself too much at home. From the 1890s onwards many landowners released this attractive North American animal on their estates as an additional amenity. The Duke of Bedford, for instance, turned some down both at Woburn Abbey in Bedfordshire, and in Regent's Park, London. When the landlord of a local pub shot seven of them in the act of feeding on a row of his peas, the Duke was much affronted.

The newcomers spread swiftly and had soon colonized the woods over a large part of southern England, and even the Inner London parks. Today the grey squirrel inhabits almost the whole of England and is frequent in most parts of Wales and in a broad belt of Central Scotland and the southern Highlands. It is often said that the grey has driven out our native red squirrel, but this is not strictly true. The red squirrel is properly an animal of coniferous forest, and in the secondary habitat of deciduous woodland which it occupies in the British Isles it is liable to big fluctuations in numbers, apparently due to disease. It so happened that at the time when the grey squirrel was first invading England the red squirrels were in a downward phase of their population cycle, so the greys found it much easier to spread than they might have if the reds had been in full force. When the reds eventually began to recover, they found the greys in possession of their former territories, and resisting their return, often by physical fighting. The greys have in fact not so much driven the reds out as prevented them from regaining a large part of their former range, with the result that the red squirrel is now almost extinct over a wide tract of central and southern England.

Grey squirrels are a serious pest in young forestry plantations, and often unwelcome in gardens, but this does not justify the epithet 'grey tree-rat' often ignorantly applied to them. They need controlling, but fortunately the authorities have been persuaded to abandon the outmoded method of offering bounties, which has been proved all over the world to be futile and to have no long-term effect on pest species.

SIKA DEER

Family: Deer Family, Cervidae.
Scientific Name: *Cervus nippon.*
Males are Stags, *Females* Hinds and
Young Calves.
Length: 5 feet.
Habitat: Woodland.
Breeding Season: Rutting, September to November. Calves born, June–July.
Antlers are cast from March to May, and grow again from May to July.
Protection: Close season for Stags: 1 May to 31 July. For Hinds: 1 March to 31 October in England and Wales; 16 February to 20 October in Scotland.
Further Reading: *Field Guide to British Deer; The Ark in Our Midst.*
(See also under *Mammals* on p. 95.)

GREY SQUIRREL

Family: Squirrel Family, Sciuridae.
Scientific name: *Sciurus carolinensis.*
Red Squirrel, *S. vulgaris.*
Nests are called Dreys.
Length: 8–9 inches.
Habitat: Woodland.
Breeding Season: Mating, December–January and April–May. Young born, February–March and July–August.
Protection: None, the animal being a classified pest.
Further Reading: *Squirrels,* by Monica Shorten (New Naturalist, 1954); *The Ark in Our Midst.*
(See also under Mammals on p. 95.)

Reindeer : Capercaillie

Visitors to Speyside nowadays have two new attractions besides the red deer, golden eagles and other traditional Highland wildlife for which the district is famous. In addition to the two pairs of ospreys (p. 36), they stand a good chance of meeting a herd of REINDEER. Since 1952 the Reindeer Council of the United Kingdom has successfully reintroduced reindeer from Lapland into Scotland. Thirty head of the present herd of thirty-eight, whose headquarters is near Aviemore, were bred in Scotland, some representing the second or third Scottish generation. This is not really surprising, because reindeer were once native to Britain, and were still being hunted in Caithness about eight hundred years ago. These reindeer were of the woodland or forest type, for Scotland was then much more heavily wooded than it is today. One reason for the failure of previous reindeer introductions in the eighteenth and nineteenth centuries was probably that the animals were mainly of the tundra type. The present herd includes animals of three different origins, Swedish woodland and mountain reindeer and the south Norwegian type.

The reindeer is unusual among deer in that both sexes bear antlers, though the cows' are smaller. During the summer the Scottish herd can be found on the high tops of Cairngorm, where they are so tame that they allow walkers to approach within a few feet to photograph them. They are, however, much troubled by inadequately controlled dogs.

Reindeer produce valuable milk, meat, hides and hair, and their antlers can also be used to carve ornaments for the tourist trade. It is hoped therefore that they will make a useful contribution to the natural resources of Scotland, for they eat lichens and other natural foods not utilized by red deer.

The CAPERCAILLIE, our largest game bird, almost the size of a small turkey, provides the most striking instance of the successful reintroduction of a bird that had become extinct in the British Isles. The last native capers appear to have been killed in Aberdeenshire in 1785, but within sixty years Swedish birds turned down in Perthshire were spreading vigorously northwards again to the Dee. Later in the century many more lairds turned down capers on their estates, with the result that this fine bird is now completely reinstated. Its present distribution ranges over the whole eastern half of the Highlands, from the southern fringes as far north as south-east Sutherland. In the west capers are only to be found around Loch Lomond, and all attempts to establish them elsewhere have so far failed, as have similar attempts in the Lowlands and in various parts of England.

The habitat most favoured by the capercaillie is the natural open type of pinewood, with plenty of heather and bilberry undergrowth. It does not really like the modern plantations of young pines, spruces and other conifers into which it is often forced by increased felling and replanting of the older type of forest. Unfortunately when capers do frequent young plantations they incur the wrath of the foresters by eating the young shoots.

REINDEER

Family: Deer Family, Cervidae.
Scientific Name: *Rangifer tarandus*.
Males are Bulls, *Females* Cows and
Young Calves.
Length: 5–6 feet, bulls larger than
cows.
Antlers are cast by bulls in December,
by cows in the spring.
Habitat: Moorland and mountain
tops.
Breeding Season: Rutting in Octo-
ber. Calves born in May.
Protection: All animals at present
are private property.
Further Reading: *Field Guide to
British Deer ; The Ark in Our Midst.*
(See also under *Mammals* on p. 95.)

CAPERCAILLIE

Family: Grouse Family, Tetraonidae.
Scientific Name: *Tetrao urogallus*.
Males are Cocks, *Females* Hens and
Young Poults.
Length: Cocks 33–35 inches, Hens
23–25 inches.
Habitat: Coniferous woods.
Breeding Season: April to June.
Protection: Close season, 1 February
to 30 September.
Further Reading: *The Ark in Our
Midst.*
(See also under *Birds* on p. 95.)

Muntjac Deer : Mandarin Duck

The MUNTJAC is a small deer no bigger than a large dog, and curiously enough derives its other name of BARKING DEER from its remarkably dog-like bark. A pair of curved, tusk-like upper canine teeth protrude from the buck's mouth.

Starting as an escape from two centres in South Bedfordshire, the muntjac has during the past sixty years or so spread over a wide area of southern England, north to Derbyshire, south to Sussex and Dorset, east to Norfolk and Suffolk and west to the Welsh Border counties. It frequents woods with plenty of brambles and other undergrowth, and is so shy and rarely seen that it may live in a district for years without most people ever becoming aware of its presence. Often the only firm indication comes from its distinctive piles of droppings.

Originally two forms of muntjac were liberated in Bedfordshire, the Indian and the smaller Chinese race. Most of the animals now at large appear to belong to the Chinese form, but some may have a certain amount of Indian blood.

Muntjac seem to be comparatively harmless new members of the British fauna, though a small amount of damage and some fraying of the bark of young trees have been reported. The fact that they are highly susceptible to hard winters, such as 1962–3, when a good many were found lying dead, suggests that they are never likely to become a really tiresome pest. This is just as well, because they are now so widespread and apparently so firmly established that it would be extremely hard to extirpate them.

The MANDARIN DUCK, as the illustration shows, is an exceedingly handsome bird, and a great acquisition to our avifauna. It is the most firmly established of the handful of alien ducks which are currently trying to establish themselves as breeding species in the British Isles; the others are the Carolina duck (p. 16) and the North American ruddy duck, which now nests every year in a few reservoirs in the Midlands and West Country.

The mandarin is well established on the borders of Surrey and Berkshire, in Windsor Great Park and especially on Virginia Water, and in a few other places. A few years ago there were estimated to be about 400 birds living ferally in the Windsor area, and at this time Peter Scott declared that the mandarin had become so rare in its native land that there might well be more birds in Windsor Great Park than in the whole of China.

The origin of the Windsor colony is obscure; its founders may either have come from a private zoological collection nearby or have descended from some which were released in the London parks around 1930 in an abortive attempt to establish a breeding colony there.

The late Lord Grey of Fallodon held that if it were not persecuted by stupid people with guns, the mandarin could and would hold its own against natural predators in any wooded area with secluded ponds or streams, and there seems little doubt that he is right. Like its relative the Carolina, the mandarin nests in holes in trees.

MUNTJAC DEER

Family: Deer Family, Cervidae.
Scientific Name: *Muntiacus muntjak.* Chinese Muntjac: *M. m. reevesi.* Indian Muntjac: *M. m. muntjak.*
Males are Bucks, *Females* Does and *Young* Fawns.
Length: $2\frac{1}{2}$–$3\frac{1}{2}$ feet.
Antlers are not shed at any definite time of year.
Habitat: Dense woodland with thick undergrowth.
Breeding Season: Rutting occurs in the winter half of the year. Fawns are born in late summer and autumn.
Protection: no close season.
Further Reading: *Field Guide to British Deer; The Ark in Our Midst.*
(See also under *Mammals* on p. 95.)

MANDARIN DUCK

Family: Duck Family, Anatidae.
Scientific Name: *Aix galericulata.*
Males are Drakes, *Females* Ducks and *Young* Ducklings.
Length: 17 inches.
Habitat: Ponds and streams in woodland, nesting in tree holes.
Breeding Season: April–May.
Protection: Throughout the year.
Further Reading: *The Mandarin Duck,* by Christopher Savage (1952); *The Ark in Our Midst; The Waterfowl of the World.*

23

Chinese Water Deer :
South African Shelduck

The CHINESE WATER DEER is the rarest and least widespread of the three or four alien species of deer which are now feral in the woods of Britain. It is quite small, about the size of a large dog or a muntjac (p. 22), and is the only species of deer in the world whose male does not bear antlers. Like the muntjac it has a pair of tusk-like teeth protruding from its mouth, but it stands a little more erect, and has a less hunched back, more rounded ears and no white around the tail.

Like the muntjac again, the Chinese water deer frequents woods, but it is also more likely to be found in reed-beds or on open farmland. At present it is known to occur in three fairly widely separated areas. In Bedfordshire, Buckinghamshire and Hertfordshire it is fairly widespread, as escapes from Whipsnade Zoo, where some were turned down about thirty-five years ago, and from Woburn Park, where some got out when the gates were left open during the war. In this area the muntjac is numerous. In North Hampshire, which muntjac are now beginning to invade, some water deer have escaped from the park at Farleigh Wallop. In Shropshire they have got into the woods from the private collection at Walcot Park; here they are still outside the muntjac's range, but the latter is spreading so fast that there is little doubt it will arrive within the next ten years or so.

The SOUTH AFRICAN SHELDUCK, also known as the GREY-HEADED SHELDUCK, is the only member of the *Casarca* group of shelducks which has nested wild in the British Isles. This group of four closely related species was formerly classed separately as the genus *Casarca,* but is now usually included in the genus *Tadorna,* to which our native British shelduck belongs. It consists of the ruddy shelduck, the South African shelduck, the New Zealand paradise shelduck and the Australian shelduck. All four are frequent in collections of ornamental waterfowl, and may be seen, for instance, at the Wildfowl Trust's collections at Slimbridge, Gloucestershire, and Peakirk, Northamptonshire.

The ruddy shelduck is the most familiar, for it breeds no further away than southern Europe, and has on occasion reached Britain as a natural vagrant. Most of the birds that turn up in various parts of the country nowadays, however, are probably escapes from wildfowl collections.

The South African shelduck differs from its ruddy relative mainly in its grey head and neck; the duck also has much more white on her head. At the outbreak of the Second World War a number were allowed to fly free from Kew Gardens and throughout the war were often seen on the adjacent foreshore of the Thames. One of these birds took up residence on a small pond on Barnes Common, Surrey, not far away, and stayed there for twelve years. After a while it was joined by a mate, and in 1946 and perhaps also in other years, this pair succeeded in rearing a brood on the Thames.

CHINESE WATER DEER

Family: Deer Family, Cervidae.
Scientific Name: *Hydropotes inermis*.
Males are Bucks, *Females* Does and
   Young Fawns.
Length: *c*.3 feet.
Antlers: None.
Habitat: Woodland, also reed-beds
   and farmland.
Breeding Season: Rutting in Decem-
   ber. Fawns born in May–June.
Protection: None.
Further Reading: *Field Guide to
   British Deer ; The Ark in Our Midst.*
(See also under *Mammals* on p. 95.)

SOUTH AFRICAN
SHELDUCK

Family: Duck Family, Anatidae.
Scientific Name: *Tadorna cana*.
   Common Shelduck: *T. tadorna*.
   Ruddy Shelduck: *T. ferruginea*.
   Paradise Shelduck: *T. variegata*.
   Australian Shelduck: *T. tadornoides*.
Males are Drakes, *Females* Ducks and
   Young Ducklings.
Length: 22 inches.
Habitat: Fresh water.
Breeding Season: Spring.
Protection: None.
Further Reading: *The Waterfowl of
   the World ; The Ark in Our Midst.*

Wild Cat : Ptarmigan

Our only native member of the Cat Family, to which lions, tigers and leopards also belong, the WILD CAT, is increasing again in the Scottish Highlands. Once inhabiting the whole island, it had become extinct in England, Wales and southern Scotland by the middle of the last century. It is doubtful if there have ever been genuine wild cats in Ireland.

By the beginning of the First World War the wild cat had reached rather a low ebb, even in the Highlands. Then, however, the absence of keepers, leading to a temporary suspension of its perennial persecution in the supposed interests of game preservation, brought about a recovery. This was quickened both by the sanctuaries provided by the increasing plantations of the Forestry Commission between the wars and by a further armistice from the gamekeepers during the Second World War. Today the wild cat is still spreading, and now occurs in all the Highland counties, though still apparently uncommon in Sutherland and Caithness. There appear, however, to be none on any of the Hebridean islands included in the county of Inverness, nor on the many islands off the coast of Argyll.

In appearance the wild cat is not unlike a fiercer domestic tabby, but it stands higher and is more thick-set, with a much bushier tail. Domestic cats gone wild often interbreed with their wild relatives, and in some parts of the Highlands there is a significant hybrid element in the wild population.

Like most mammal predators the wild cat takes what prey it can get, and although its feeding habits have not been studied scientifically, it seems clear that it eats mainly mice, voles, shrews and small birds. Naturally sportsmen focus attention on the fact that it sometimes also competes with them by taking grouse, mountain hares, rabbits and roe fawns, but modern studies of the important part played by predators in maintaining the health and vigour of wild animal populations do not countenance the view that this is a good reason for persecuting the wild cat.

The PTARMIGAN, one of our five native resident game birds, is also our only bird to spend its entire life high up on the tops of mountains, where its largely white winter plumage helps to protect it during the winter snows. It is at present confined to the Highlands of Scotland, including both Skye and Mull, though in the last century it was more widespread, south to the Lake District and west to the Outer Isles. Attempts to reintroduce the ptarmigan to areas where it has become extinct, especially in the Southern Uplands of Scotland, have so far all ended in failure, perhaps because too few birds have been released.

On Deeside ptarmigan breed down to 2,700 ft, staying in winter as high up the hill as the snow permits. Further west they come down to 2,000 ft in Wester Ross, and as low as 600 ft in the far north-west of Sutherland, where the mountain plants also descend to sea-level. The food of the ptarmigan consists almost entirely of the shoots, leaves and stems of such plants as ling heather, crowberry and blaeberry, the last being the Scots name for the bilberry of northern England and the whortleberry of the south.

WILD CAT

Family: Cat Family, Felidae.
Scientific Name: *Felis silvestris.*
Young are Kittens.
Length: 33–40 inches.
Habitat: Woods, moors and mountains.
Breeding Season: Kittens born in May.
Protection: None.
Further Reading: See under *Mammals* on p. 95.

PTARMIGAN

Family: Grouse Family, Tetraonidae.
Scientific Name: *Lagopus mutus.*
Males are Cocks, *Females* Hens and *Young* Poults.
Length: 13–14 inches.
Habitat: High moors and mountain tops.
Breeding Season: May to July.
Protection: Close season, 11 December to 11 August.
Further Reading: See under *Birds* on p. 95.

Pine Marten : Crossbill

The handsome PINE MARTEN, an outsize warm chestnut-brown stoat, is almost the only British mammal which has been in any danger of extinction in recent years. Once widespread in woods almost throughout the British Isles, it is confined today to the north-western Highlands of Scotland, the English Lake District, the Snowdonia region of North Wales, and parts of Ireland, where it may be more frequent than published records suggest. After more than a hundred years of severe persecution in the supposed interests of game preservation, the pine marten has since the Second World War shown signs of recovery, especially in the Highlands. Within the past few years a number have been seen south of the Caledonian Canal. Odd individuals have been seen much further afield, but most of these had probably escaped from captivity.

Even where it is most frequent, in the wilder glens of Sutherland, for instance, or in the Beinn Eighe national nature reserve in Wester Ross, the pine marten is very rarely seen. Like most British mammals it is largely nocturnal in habit, so that much the best chance of seeing one is within an hour or two of sunrise or sunset. Mice, voles and small birds form the great bulk of its diet, though no doubt squirrels are sometimes taken too, as in Sweden, where one recent study showed that half the marten's winter prey consisted of red squirrels. It is hard, therefore, to understand why in the past game-keepers should have made such a dead set at this attractive animal.

The CROSSBILL is unique among British birds in having the mandibles of its bill crossed, the better to enable it to extract from pine and spruce cones the seeds which form its principal food. Not surprisingly, it is rarely found away from these or other coniferous trees, such as larch and fir. Cock crossbills are most handsome birds, with their predominantly red plumage, and a party of crossbills feeding, with the flashes of red, and of yellowish-green from the hens, as the birds dart about from cone to cone, is one of the most attractive sights a British bird watcher can hope to see.

There are two quite distinct breeding groups of crossbills in the British Isles. In England crossbills breed regularly only in the pine and sand country of the East Anglian Breckland, around Thetford and Brandon. Every few years, however, there is an invasion or irruption from some part of Scandinavia where the spruce crop has failed, and then a few pairs often nest in other districts that are well provided with conifers, while non-breeding birds may be widespread. In the Scottish Highlands, on the other hand, there is a resident form with a slightly larger bill, and this is now believed by the experts to be a form of the North European parrot-crossbill.

The crossbill has an unusually early breeding season, and may start as early as January. Needless to say, its nest is invariably built on a conifer.

PINE MARTEN

Family: Stoat Family, Mustelidae.
Scientific Name: *Martes martes*.
Length: 25–32 inches.
Habitat: Woods and rocky moorland.
Breeding Season: Young born, March–April.
Protection: None.
Further Reading: See under *Mammals* on p. 95.

CROSSBILL

Family: Finch Family, Fringillidae.
Scientific name: Common Crossbill, *Loxia curvirostra*. Scottish Crossbill, *L. pytyopsittacus*.
Males are Cocks, *Females* Hens.
Length: 6½ inches.
Habitat: Coniferous woodland, and areas with scattered conifers.
Breeding Season: January to July, but mostly February in England and March in Scotland.
Protection: Throughout the year (in England and Wales, with special penalties).
Further Reading: See under *Birds* on p. 95.

29

Polecat : Chough

The POLECAT, like the pine marten (p. 28), an outsize stoat, has had the ill fortune to get into a proverb based on the foetid smell of its anal gland secretion. In days gone by this reputation for evil-smelling earned it the folk-name of foumart or foulmart, as distinct from the sweetmart, which was the pine marten.

Since the polecat has an unfortunate taste for young poultry and game birds, it has always been highly unpopular with farmers and game preservers, and so from being widespread throughout the British Isles has been driven back into the fastnesses of Central Wales. Smaller numbers occur elsewhere in Wales, and perhaps also in Devon, Cornwall and the Lake District, but in Scotland it is almost certainly extinct. From time to time polecats are reported from other parts of the British Isles, but the great majority of these are undoubtedly escaped polecat-ferrets. Zoologists wrangle endlessly about the origin and relationship of the ferret and the polecat-ferret, but for practical purposes a ferret is a domesticated albino polecat and a polecat-ferret is a domesticated normal dark-coloured polecat and so, of course, remarkably hard to tell from a polecat in the field. On the Isle of Mull a population of feral polecat-ferrets has been at large for some years.

While polecats clearly cannot be encouraged in the immediate neighbourhood of poultry farms, they are important members of our carnivorous fauna, which before the myxomatosis epidemic of 1954-5 played their part in keeping down that serious agricultural pest the rabbit, and certainly should not be allowed to become extinct.

The CHOUGH is easily recognized as an all-black crow with red bill and legs, even without hearing the high-pitched call that gives the bird its onomatopoeic name. Once known as the Cornish chough, and indeed still a feature of that county's heraldic arms, the chough is now alas virtually extinct in its last haunts on the north coast of Cornwall. In Scotland too it has become very rare, extinct on the mainland and confined to Islay, Jura and one or two others of the Inner Hebrides. Fortunately, however, it survives on the coast of Pembrokeshire, in a few places in North Wales, and in the Isle of Man, while in parts of Ireland it is still quite common, replacing the jackdaw on some western cliffs.

That Gilbert White of Selborne should have been able to write that Cornish choughs 'abound and breed on Beachy-head and on all the cliffs of the Sussex coast' shows how much the bird has decreased over the past two hundred years or so. Nobody has been able to suggest the cause of the decline, though the jackdaw has been accused of being the villain of the piece. It seems more likely, however, that as with the grey and red squirrels, the jackdaw has merely moved in after some unknown factor had reduced the number of choughs.

The chough is one of the most clearly neutral or beneficial birds in the British avifauna, its known food consisting of dung and other beetles, grasshoppers, earthworms, crustaceans, molluscs, spiders and lizards.

POLECAT

Family: Stoat Family, Mustelidae.
Scientific Name: *Mustela putorius.*
Length: 20–24 inches.
Habitat: Woods and moorland.
Breeding Season: April–May.
Protection: None.
Further Reading: See under *Mammals* on page 95.

CHOUGH

Family: Crow Family, Corvidae.
Scientific Name: *Pyrrhocorax pyrrhocorax.*
Length: 15 inches.
Habitat: Sea and inland cliffs.
Breeding Season: April to June.
Protection: Throughout the year, with special penalties.
Further Reading: See under *Birds* on p. 95.

Mink : Rainbow Trout

The MINK is the latest comer among our larger introduced fauna, but bids fair to become as firmly established as any of them before long. It is barely ten years since the mink was first proved to be breeding ferally in Britain, on the upper reaches of the River Teign on the edge of Dartmoor, yet already it is well established in Hampshire, Wiltshire, three Welsh counties and north-eastern Scotland, and shows every sign of spreading farther.

The American mink—for there is also a European species—is, like both pine marten and polecat, an outsize stoat in appearance. It has long been trapped for its fine fur in North America, and has also been kept on fur farms in various parts of Britain. It is escapes from some of these farms which have begun breeding here, and so have produced what is potentially the most serious pest that has been let loose on the unsuspecting British public since the muskrat also escaped from fur farms. In Iceland, where mink escaped and spread some years ago, they have decimated the breeding wildfowl, and there is every reason to suppose that they will do the same in Britain, as well as raiding chicken farms with weak defences. In America they feed largely on aquatic mammals— so the water vole had better look out!—but also on fish. Water bailiffs are unlikely to welcome the appearance of mink on their streams, but the potential damage to fish is likely to be less than to wildfowl.

Sooner or later a British-bred mink will, as in the illustration, catch and eat a RAINBOW TROUT, another naturalized species from North America. The first rainbow trout to reach Britain from their native Pacific coast were a batch of 3,000 sent to a trout hatchery on the Buckinghamshire Colne in 1884. They soon became popular, and were widely distributed in lakes and streams throughout the British Isles, from Buckingham Palace grounds to Lochbuie on the Isle of Mull. Later on complaints began to be heard that they were driving out the native brown trout. Eventually Dr Barton Worthington, then director of the freshwater laboratory on Lake Windermere, was asked to investigate. His report in 1939 listed the comparatively few rivers and lakes where rainbows were actually breeding and maintaining themselves: among them Blagdon Reservoir in Somerset, the River Wye in Derbyshire, a lake at Newstead Abbey in Nottinghamshire, and parts of several small rivers in Cambridgeshire, Rutland, Kent and the Chilterns. Of course, there were a great many more lakes and rivers where attempts to establish rainbow trout had failed.

The most fascinating story Dr Worthington had to tell was the way the rainbows had managed to establish themselves in the Derbyshire Wye from just above Bakewell to its confluence with the Derwent. This was one of the rivers where the incomer stood accused of driving out the brown trout, despite extensive restocking. However, when the problem was examined scientifically, the real villain proved to be the town of Buxton, whose sewage was polluting the river. This was killing off the brown trout, but the tougher rainbows were able to stand up to it.

MINK

Family: Stoat Family, Mustelidae.
Scientific Name: American Mink, *Mustela vison*. European Mink, *M. lutreola*.
Length: 17–26 inches.
Habitat: By freshwater lakes, rivers and streams.
Breeding Season: Spring.
Protection: None.
Further Reading: *The Ark in Our Midst.*
(See also under *Mammals* on p. 95.)

RAINBOW TROUT

Family: Salmon Family, Salmonidae.
Scientific Name: *Salmo gairdnerii*, Brown trout, *S. trutta*.
Length: Up to 30 inches.
Habitat: Freshwater lakes and rivers.
Breeding Season: Spring.
Protection: Close season, September to February.
Further Reading: *The Ark in Our Midst.*
(See also under *Fishes* on p. 95.)

33

Common Carp : Crucian Carp : Ide : Golden Orfe

The COMMON CARP (centre front), a native of Asia from the regions around the Black and Caspian Seas eastwards through Turkestan to China, is today widespread in lakes, ponds and slow-moving streams in the British Isles, preferring those with muddy bottoms. We do not know exactly when it was first introduced to Britain, whether, for instance, the Romans brought it with them. The earliest written evidence we have is in *The Boke of St Albans*, a kind of late fifteenth century sporting encyclopaedia said to have been written by Dame Juliana Berners, a lady whose authorship and even existence are in as much doubt as Homer's. At all events the *Boke* tells us that the carp is 'a daynteous fysshe, but there ben fewe in Englonde'. Eric Taverner has suggested that the carp was in fact first imported to England from the Low Countries in the fourteenth century and bred in monastic and other stewponds. Once they were here, it was easy enough to transport carp about the country, for they travel well wrapped in wet moss or waterweeds. Carp appear not to have reached Ireland before the reign of King James I.

Carp grow to a substantial size, up to 20–25 lb., and are reputed also to live to a great age, an assertion that cannot yet be substantiated by exact records. The mirror carp is a variety of the common carp that has only a few rows of large scales, and the leather carp another variety with no scales at all.

The CRUCIAN CARP (bottom), on the other hand, is not a variety of the common carp, as is sometimes suggested, but an entirely distinct and native species, smaller and lacking the common carp's distinctive barbels. It does, however, resemble the common species in preferring still or slow-moving muddy waters, and in being easily transportable in wet moss. Its curious name derives from the German *Karausche*.

Hitherto there has been very little reliable information on the distribution of the crucian carp in British rivers, but a survey by David Marlborough in the January 1966 issue of *The Naturalist* shows clearly that it is mainly a fish of the English lowlands. It is widespread in the south and Midlands, extending north to the southern parts of Lancashire and Yorkshire, and west to Hampshire, Wiltshire and Somerset, and being most frequently reported in the Thames, East Anglian and Mersey regions. In Wales the crucian carp is very local, having been recently reported only from Glamorgan and Denbigh. The ranges of all the larger freshwater fish in Britain are highly artificial, owing to the stocking activities of anglers, and the crucian carp is no exception.

The IDE (centre, back) is a North European freshwater fish, closely related to the dace and chub, which has been introduced into various British waters, but much less often than its varieties the GOLDEN ORFE (top) and silver orfe. Golden orfe breed freely throughout England and southern Scotland, but as they have not as yet spread by natural means away from the ponds where they have been introduced, they must be regarded as acclimatized rather than naturalized.

34

ALL FOUR

Family: Carp Family, Cyprinidae.
Protection: Close season, March to June.
Further Reading: *The Ark in Our Midst.*
(See also under *Fishes* on p. 95.)

COMMON CARP

Scientific Name: *Cyprinus carpio.*
Length: Up to 3 feet.
Habitat: Lakes, ponds and slow-moving streams, especially with muddy bottoms.
Breeding Season: May–June.

CRUCIAN CARP

Scientific Name: *Carassius carassius.*
Length: Up to 15 inches.
Habitat: As for common carp.
Breeding Season: May to July.

IDE AND GOLDEN ORFE

Scientific Name: *Leuciscus idus.*
Length: About 12 inches.
Habitat: Artificial lakes and ponds.
Breeding Season: April–May.

Osprey : Char

The return of the OSPREY to breed in Scotland is one of the great triumphs of bird protection in Britain since the war, just as its decline throughout the last century and eventual extinction early in the present one were grave blots on the escutcheon of the naturalists of those years. For some reason the osprey, that magnificent fishing hawk—no connection with the plumes known as 'osprey', which come from egrets—has always attracted the especial attentions of the more anti-social egg collectors. It was they who pursued it to extinction, one egg thief even going to the length of swimming naked over to its island eyrie on Loch an Eilein, its last haunt on Speyside, to commit his crime. The ospreys that nested on Loch Arkaig in 1908 and on Loch Loyne in 1916 were the last of the indigenous Scottish race. Those that have recolonized the Highlands during the past ten years probably hail from Scandinavia, where the osprey is still comparatively common.

During the early 1950s there were persistent reports that ospreys were once again nesting in Scotland, but not until 1955 were they definitely proved to be doing so, in Strathspey. For the next few years a single pair tried and failed to breed each year, their efforts culminating in a nocturnal smash-and-grab raid by an unknown kleptomaniac under the very eyes of the watchers appointed by the Royal Society for the Protection of Birds. After that the Society organized the annual guarding of the ospreys' eyrie with almost military precision, and since 1959 have been rewarded by one pair nesting successfully almost annually. More recently a second pair has been present, but so far there have never been two successful nests in the same year.

The osprey undoubtedly eats fish, especially pike and trout, but a few pairs of these splendid birds are hardly likely seriously to diminish trout stocks in the Highlands, and may even help to improve them. In any case most fly fishermen are glad to see their 'rival' and do not grudge him his catches.

In the past ospreys doubtless occasionally caught CHAR, as shown in the illustration, though we have no evidence that any of the new generation have done so yet. The char is a relative of the salmon found in cold, deep, mountain lakes and lochs, where it is rarely seen, for it comes to the surface to feed only in the evenings. Isolated in their mountain fastnesses, the char of each lake have evolved slight differences which have led a few zoologists to regard them all as distinct species. Certainly many of them have their own local names.

In England there are char in Lakes Windermere and Haweswater in the Lake District. In Wales the char is called the torgoch and is found in two lakes at the foot of Snowdon, and perhaps also one in Merioneth. In Scotland the char of Loch Killin in Inverness-shire is called the haddy, and there are also char in two lochs in Sutherland and one in Shetland; the Orkney char appears to be extinct. Ireland boasts no fewer than seven distinct forms of char, including the extinct 'whiting' of Lough Neagh.

OSPREY

Family: Hawk Family, Accipitridae.
Scientific Name: *Pandion haliaetus.*
Length: 20–23 inches, females larger than males.
Habitat: Freshwater lochs.
Breeding Season: April to July.
Protection: Throughout the year, with special penalties.
Further Reading: *The Return of the Osprey*, by Philip Brown and George Waterston (1962).
(See also under *Birds* on p. 95.)

CHAR

Family: Salmon Family, Salmonidae.
Scientific Name: *Salvelinus alpinus.* Torgoch, *S. a. perisii.* Haddy, *S. a. killinensis.* Windermere Char, *S. a. willughbii.* Haweswater Char, *S. a. lonsdalii.* Shetland Char, *S. a. gracillimus.* Orkney Char, *S. a. inframundus.*
Length: 6–18 inches.
Habitat: Deep mountain lochs and tarns.
Breeding Season: November to February.
Protection: Close season, September to February.
Further Reading: See under *Fishes* on p. 95.)

Golden Eagle

This most magnificent of our birds of prey, while it cannot properly be described as rare, is very far from being common, even in the Highlands of Scotland, and unfortunately now appears to be decreasing. About ten years ago two separate estimates put the number of breeding pairs of GOLDEN EAGLES in Scotland at 180–190. Since then there have been most disturbing reports of low breeding success, apparently as a result of the pollution of the environment by pesticide residues, and the total number of breeding pairs has probably fallen.

Two hundred years ago the golden eagle also bred in North Wales—Snowdon's Welsh name, Eryri, is said to refer to an eagle's eyrie—the English Lake and Peak Districts, the Cheviots, the Galloway hills and several parts of Ireland. That it had been driven back into the Highlands by the end of the last century is a tribute to the misguided vigour with which gamekeepers and others have persecuted it. In recent years, however, the eagle has been trying to recolonize some of these lost territories, and has bred in Galloway and Northern Ireland and been seen in the Lake District.

It was in 1964 that Drs Lockie and Ratcliffe of the Nature Conservancy published their alarming report which showed that over a wide area of the western Highlands the proportion of golden eagle pairs rearing young had fallen from nearly three-quarters in 1937–60 to less than one-third in 1961–3. Ten eggs from seven eyries proved to be contaminated with chlorinated hydrocarbons, pesticide residues which were probably mainly responsible for the decline. The eagles probably come by these residues through eating sheep carrion, the sheep themselves having absorbed the poison into their fat, flesh and fleeces while being dipped. As a result of this and other reports, an official ban has been placed on the use of dieldrin in sheep dips. It is noteworthy that on Deeside, where there are many deer forests, and the eagles eat much less sheep carrion, a higher proportion of pairs continue to rear their young successfully.

Indeed golden eagles are generally much commoner on deer forests, where they are not persecuted but welcomed because they prey on grouse, whose warning cackle may disturb the deer just as they are being carefully stalked. In fact, although golden eagles do eat grouse, they prefer rabbits and hares when they can find them. Moreover, the recent research of Dr David Jenkins and his Nature Conservancy team suggests that even when golden eagles do eat grouse they have very little influence on the number of breeding pairs each spring. All they and other grouse predators appear to do is to mop up the surplus individuals which have not been able to find territories of their own.

An adult golden eagle is dark golden brown all over, sometimes with a pale head, but young birds, which are the most likely to wander southwards into England in winter, have a white tail with a black bar at its square tip. This reverses the plumages of the rare white-tailed or sea eagle, a former breeding species, whose adult has a white wedge-shaped tail with no black bar, while the juvenile's tail is all dark brown.

GOLDEN EAGLE

Family: Hawk Family, Accipitridae.
Scientific Name: *Aquila chrysaëtos.*
Sea Eagle, *Haliaeëtus albicilla.*
Young are Eaglets, the *Nest Site* an
Eyrie.
Length: 30–35 inches, females larger
than males.
Habitat: Mountains and moorland.
Breeding Season: March to July.
Protection: Throughout the year,
with special penalties.
Further Reading: *The Golden Eagle,*
by Seton Gordon (1955); *Eagles,* by
Leslie Brown (1955).
(See also under *Birds* on p. 95.)

39

Roller : Bath White

The ROLLER is one of our most striking rarities, with its blue-green plumage, offset by a chestnut back and also, when it flies, by a brilliant blue flash in the wings. It is a bird more familiar to ornithologists in East Africa, where three kinds of roller perch on posts and bush tops on the look-out for large flying insects; our own European species in its winter quarters and two handsome African ones, the lilac-breasted and the rufous-crowned. The handful of rollers that appear in Britain in most years have probably overshot the mark when migrating northwards to the Mediterranean coast of France, which is the nearest part of their breeding range to the British Isles.

During the seven years since the Rarity Records Committee began to produce annual reports in the journal *British Birds,* rollers have been reliably reported on a dozen occasions, but not every year. They have been widely spread over the British Isles, from Staines on the western outskirts of London to Castlegregory in Co. Kerry and North-mavine in Shetland. Rollers are most often seen in May or June, but a few also in July and the autumn, and occasionally one has stayed for several weeks in the same district.

The roller is an insect-eating bird, feeding on a wide variety of larger invertebrates, including beetles, locusts, spiders, centipedes and ants. It frequents areas with scattered trees and nests usually in a tree-hole, but also in holes in walls and buildings. Its name comes from its curious tumbling courtship display flight, in which the male turns somersaults in the air.

The BATH WHITE is one of our rarest butterflies, by no means seen in every year. A native of central and southern Europe, at long intervals it reaches Britain in some numbers, as in 1872, when thirty-five were captured, and 1945, when there was a fantastic invasion all along the south coast from Kent to Cornwall in July, and six or seven weeks later a second brood began to appear from eggs laid by the first on wild mignonette and hedge mustard. A very few even appeared the following spring, having overwintered as chrysalids. There was evidently another invasion in 1906, when a good many freshly emerged specimens were seen during August on the cliffs at Lulworth Cove, Dorset. In other years only odd specimens have been seen.

The Bath white owes its name to the fact that it featured in a piece of needlework executed by a young lady of that city in the eighteenth century; the specimen she used as model was said to have been taken near Bath. To the butterfly hunters of that day it was more picturesquely known as the Greenish half mourner, or Vernon's half mourner, from the fact that a specimen, which still exists in the collection of the Hope Department of the University of Oxford, was taken in Cambridgeshire in May 1702 by a Mr Vernon.

Our other rare white butterfly is the black-veined white, which until quite recently was thought to have become extinct in the 1920s, but has recently been rediscovered in Kent.

ROLLER

Family: Roller Family, Coraciidae.
Scientific Name: *Coracias garrulus*.
  Lilac-breasted Roller, *C. caudata*.
  Rufous-crowned Roller, *C. naevia*.
Length: 12 inches.
Habitat: Parkland and other open
  country with scattered trees.
Breeding Season: Has never bred in
  Britain.
Protection: Throughout the year,
  with special penalties.
Further Reading: See under *Birds*
  on p. 95.

BATH WHITE

Family: White Family, Pieridae.
Scientific Name: *Pontia daplidice*.
  Black-veined White, *Aporia crataegi*.
Wing-span: 1¾ inches.
Habitat: Open country, sometimes in
  fields of lucerne.
On the Wing: July to September.
Protection: None.
Further Reading: See under *Butter-*
  flies on p. 95.

41

Little Owl : Large Copper

The LITTLE OWL, our smallest owl, and also the most familiar, since it flies by day as well as in the dusk, is no native but an incomer from the Continent. First unsuccessfully introduced by that magnificent eccentric Charles Waterton in Yorkshire in 1842, it was more than forty years before, after several more false starts, Lord Lilford managed to get a feral population breeding on his Northamptonshire estate. Others followed his example, and by 1900 little owls were also breeding in Kent, Rutland and Bedfordshire. Then the invasion really began. By 1910 they were west to the Severn estuary and north to the Trent, and ten years later almost everywhere south of the Humber, except in North Wales, Devon and Cornwall. By 1930 even these strongholds were conquered, and in the next ten years the little owl was reaching north towards the Scottish Border, though it was not actually proved to breed in Scotland until 1958. Today over most of England and Wales the little owl has become appreciably scarcer than it was thirty years ago, almost certainly partly due to the fell effect of pesticide residues, which have also decimated kestrels, sparrowhawks and other birds of prey both large and small.

Scarcely was the little owl firmly established in the vacant ecological niche that existed in our countryside for a small, diurnal and mainly insectivorous bird of prey, than a howl of protest went up from the game-preserving community. Just because it had a hooked beak and occasionally ate a game chick, it was accused of almost every crime in the calendar. The upshot was a vindication by one of the earliest field inquiries of the British Trust for Ornithology, which showed that its diet consisted almost exclusively of mice, voles, small song-birds, snails, slugs, earthworms, beetles and other insects. This eventually led to the complete protection of this useful bird by Act of Parliament. Nowadays both country dwellers and countrygoers welcome the occasional sight of this attractive little bird, often sitting bolt upright on a tree or pole, and making curious bobbing motions if it is too closely examined, before flying off with its low, dipping flight.

The handsome LARGE COPPER butterfly was exterminated by a combination of drainage of its habitat with the rapacity of collectors anxious to fill their cabinets before it became extinct. Its career as a known British insect was sadly short. First discovered in the fens of Huntingdonshire at the very end of the eighteenth century, it had already become very rare by 1835. Within another dozen years the last of our native stock was captured at Holme Fen, Huntingdonshire. An attempt to reintroduce the Continental race at Wicken Fen, Cambridgeshire, in 1909 failed, although another in Co. Tipperary succeeded at first, some surviving for many years. A further effort was then made at Woodwalton Fen, Huntingdonshire, in May 1930, with larvae of the newly discovered race *batavus* from Friesland, and this colony persists, with the aid of a certain amount of nursing. To make it possible, a large quantity of the larva's food plant, great water dock, had to be planted in the Fen.

LITTLE OWL

Family: Owl Family, Strigidae.
Scientific Name: *Athene noctua.*
Young owls are owlets.
Length: 9 inches.
Habitat: Farmland and other country
  with scattered trees.
Breeding Season: April to July.
Protection: Throughout the year.
Further Reading: *Report of the Little
  Owl Food Inquiry,* by Alice Hibbert-
  Ware (1938); *The Ark in Our Midst.*
  (See also under *Birds* on p. 95.)

LARGE COPPER

Family: Copper Family, Lycaenidae.
Scientific Name: *Lycaena dispar.*
Wing-span: $1\frac{3}{4}$ inches.
Habitat: Fens.
On the Wing: June–July.
Food-plant: Great Water Dock,
  Rumex hydrolapathum.
Protection: Completely protected, as
  Woodwalton Fen is now a national
  nature reserve.
Further Reading: See under *Butter-
  flies on* p. 95.

Snowy Owl

The magnificent SNOWY OWL, a rare winter visitor mainly to the northern parts of Britain, is twice the size of our only other white owl, the barn owl. Its plumage is all-white, except for some blackish-brown bars and speckles, whereas the barn owl is white only on the face and underparts, its back and wings being normally a warm gingery brown. Nevertheless the two still do occasionally get confused, particularly when, as happened in the Chilterns a few years ago, an albino or partially albino barn owl turns up.

At the beginning of the last century the snowy owl was a regular winter visitor in some numbers to the Shetlands. By the 1860s, however, it had already become scarce, at least partly because so many were shot to meet the demands of greedy collectors in the south. One crofter alone claimed to have shot at least thirty snowy owls in the period up to 1871. After this the snowy owl became a rare bird, and in the first half of the present century only five were recorded. Latterly, however, there has been a slight increase, and one was present in Shetland in the summer of 1963, and again from February to November 1964. This does not mean that there is any prospect of it starting to nest; apparently in the old days summering birds were not infrequent. Snowy owls are sometimes kept in captivity, and suspicion of being an escape must therefore attach to such southern records as the bird that was seen in Essex for three weeks in March 1963, and even to the one which stayed in the Isles of Scilly in the winter of 1964–5.

The snowy owl is circumpolar in its distribution, and our birds doubtless come from Scandinavia, or perhaps from Iceland, where a few pairs are resident. Its staple diet in both Scandinavia and Arctic Canada is lemmings, and the numbers of owls fluctuate with the well-known ups and downs of the lemming population.

Four other species of owl also occur as rare visitors to Britain. Much the largest, even larger than the snowy owl, is the eared eagle owl, which is also much kept in captivity, so that the great majority of recent occurrences are open to the suspicion of being escapes. This may well not have applied, however, to the pair seen by the late Duke of Bedford at Cairnsmore, Kirkcudbrightshire, during the late spring and early summer of 1941. In Sweden, where it is decreasing owing to human persecution, the eagle owl feeds mainly on rats and smaller rodents, but also on birds.

The earless hawk owl is another rarity that was much more frequent in the last century; in the present one it has occurred only twice, in 1903 and 1959. It is another circumpolar species, a few of the British specimens that have been positively identified proving to belong to the North American race.

Our two other rare owls are both small, about the size of a little owl (p. 42): the earless Tengmalm's owl from northern Europe and the eared scops owl from the Mediterranean.

SNOWY OWL

Family: Owl Family, Strigidae.

Scientific Name: *Nyctea scandiaca.* Eagle Owl, *Bubo bubo.* Hawk Owl, *Surnia ulula.* Tengmalm's Owl, *Aegolius funereus.* Scops Owl, *Otus scops.*

Length: 21–24 inches, females larger than males.

Habitat: Open moorland.

Breeding Season: Has never bred in Britain.

Protection: Throughout the year.

Further Reading: See under *Birds* on p. 95.

45

Short-eared Owl : Snow Goose

The SHORT-EARED OWL is not a rare bird in the same sense as the snowy owl, though it is certainly scarce compared with the tawny, barn and little owls. Its short 'ears', actually tufts of feathers, are rarely seen. The short-eared owl habitually flies in the daytime, and is in fact much the most likely large brown owl to be seen flying before sunset or after sunrise, for the much commoner tawny owl is rarely voluntarily on the wing before dusk. An additional distinction at close range is the colour of the eyes: golden-yellow in the short-eared, and black in the tawny.

In Britain the short-eared owl is primarily a winter visitor, and in parts of eastern England is known as the woodcock owl because it arrives at about the same time as the woodcock. From autumn round to early spring, it is fairly widespread in small numbers in open country throughout the British Isles, especially on moorland, downland and near the sea on sand dunes and saltmarshes. It is a bird one might expect to see, for instance, on a five-mile walk along the sea walls of the Essex coast, or along the Berkshire Ridgeway, or on the moors of the Scottish Border.

In the breeding season the short-eared owl is much more localized, though even then not really rare; it is well established in Orkney, for instance, and nests regularly. Its distribution at this time is largely governed by the abundance of voles, and when there is a plague of these, as in the Scottish Border hills in 1934, several pairs may breed in a tract of country that normally holds at most one pair. In most years scattered pairs of short-eared owls may be found nesting in the hill country of Scotland and northern England, and more locally in East Anglia and West Wales.

The SNOW GOOSE is one of our rarer geese, but does in fact visit the British Isles almost annually. It has three distinct forms, of which only two, the greater and lesser snow geese, are pure white as in the illustration. The third form is the blue snow goose, blue-grey above and usually also below, which was once believed to be a separate species but is now regarded as a colour phase of the lesser snow goose. This is a case of what scientists call dimorphism, of a bird having two distinct colour forms, such as is also found with the dark and light forms of the arctic skua, and more widely in other groups of animals.

The breeding grounds of the blue snow goose were long a mystery, and it was not until 1929 that they were first found by J. D. Soper on Baffin Island, alongside a colony of lesser snow geese. In the British Isles blue snow geese are most often seen with the great flock of Greenland white-fronted geese that frequents Wexford Slob in south-eastern Ireland. The two pure white forms appear most frequently in Scotland, usually with flocks of grey geese, the greater snow goose being much the rarer. However, a warning needs to be uttered that not every white goose is a snow goose. Our regular species of grey geese not infrequently produce albinos, and if you do correctly identify a snow goose by its black wing-tips, it is, especially in the south, almost as likely to be an escape from a wildfowl collection as a genuine wild bird.

SHORT-EARED OWL

Family: Owl Family, Strigidae.
Scientific Name: *Asio flammeus*.
Tawny Owl, *Strix aluco*.
Young owls are Owlets.
Length: 15 inches.
Habitat: Open country, downs, moors, marshes, fens, dunes and saltmarshes.
Breeding Season: April to June or July, depending on the supply of voles.
Protection: Throughout the year.
Further Reading: See under *Birds* on p. 95.

SNOW GOOSE

Family: Duck Family, Anatidae.
Scientific Name: *Anser caerulescens*. Lesser Snow Goose and Blue Snow Goose, *A. c. caerulescens*. Greater Snow Goose, *A. c. atlanticus*.
Males are Ganders, *Females* Geese.
Length: Lesser and Blue: 25–28 inches. Greater: 30 inches.
Habitat: Coastal marshes and farmland.
Breeding Season: Has never bred in Britain.
Protection: Throughout the year.
Further Reading: *The Waterfowl of the World*.
(See also under *Birds* on p. 95.)

47

Canada Goose : Coypu

The CANADA GOOSE is one of the half dozen most firmly established of our introduced birds, and has been far the most successful of the various alien waterfowl that have been allowed to fly free from ornamental waters in Britain. Canada geese were kept in captivity as long ago as the reign of King Charles II, but it was apparently not until the beginning of the last century that they began to establish themselves in the wild. Today there are some three thousand breeding pairs in various parts of Great Britain, from the south coast of England north to the shores of the Moray Firth. The strongest colonies are to be found on the meres in the East Anglian Breckland, various artificial lakes and other waters in the Thames valley in Berkshire, the meres of Cheshire and Shropshire, the Dukeries in Nottinghamshire, and in Scotland on Loch Leven, Kinross-shire. There are also many smaller colonies, especially since the Wildfowl Trust and the Wildfowlers' Association started their translocation scheme, whereby geese from waters where landowners found their increasing numbers an embarrassment were rounded up during the flightless period of their moult and removed to other waters where they were more welcome.

The Canada goose has a black-and-white face pattern somewhat similar to the much more local barnacle goose, which is a winter visitor, but its greater size and generally ash-brown plumage should preclude confusion. In its native North America there are many races of the Canada goose, of varying size, but so far as is known all the British stocks descend from the largest race, which inhabits eastern Canada. Although it is probable that a few genuinely wild Canada geese do sometimes stray across the Atlantic, especially to the Western Isles, this is naturally now very hard to prove.

The COYPU is the only South American animal that has ever successfully established itself in the British Isles, and it is one of the comparatively few that have become pests, so that expensive steps have had to be taken to eradicate them. Known to the fur trade as nutria, the coypu is a large otter-sized aquatic rodent that began to be kept on fur farms in Britain about thirty-five years ago. Quite soon escapes were reported, and by the time the authorities found time to look into the position in 1943, coypus were well established in both the Norfolk Broads and a sewage farm in the Thames valley near Slough. No action was taken at the time, for there was no evidence that they were doing any damage, but within ten years they began to spread rapidly from their Broadland sanctuary along the river valleys of East Anglia, Cambridgeshire and Essex. At the same time some damage to crops was reported, and the Ministry of Agriculture was obliged to start a campaign against the invader, as it had done against the muskrat thirty years before. Now the coypu is once more penned back into its Broadland stronghold whence, informed opinion holds, it is unlikely ever to be eradicated. No other colonies are known in Great Britain at present, except perhaps still in the Thames valley.

CANADA GOOSE

Family: Duck Family, Anatidae.
Scientific Name: *Branta canadensis.*
Males are Ganders, *Females* Geese and
    Young Goslings.
Length : 36–40 inches.
·**Habitat:** Freshwater lakes, in winter
    sometimes on the coast.
Breeding Season: April–May.
Protection: Close season, 21 Febru-
    ary to 31 August.
Further Reading: *The Waterfowl of
    the World ; The Ark in Our Midst.*
    (See also under *Birds* on p. 95.)

COYPU

Family: Capromyidae.
Scientific Name: *Myocastor coypus.*
Length: 27–29 inches.
Habitat: Reed-beds and freshwater
    margins in the Norfolk Broads.
Breeding Season: Throughout the
    year.
Protection: None; a scheduled pest.
Further Reading: *The Ark in Our
    Midst.*
(See also under *Mammals* on p. 95.)

49

4

Goosander : Goldeneye : Smew

All three of the handsome ducks on this plate are winter visitors to Britain, though the goosander also breeds in the north. None of them can be called rare, though the smew is very local.

The GOOSANDER (centre) is the largest of our three sawbills, so named from the serrated edge of their bills, an adaptation to help them catch fish; the two others are the red-breasted merganser and smew. In spring and summer the goosander breeds, usually in a hole in a tree, by freshwater lochs and rivers over a wide area of the Scottish Highlands; in the Lowlands it is more local, and only comparatively recently has it begun to spread over the Border into northern England. The red-breasted merganser has a very similar breeding range, but also nests by sea lochs and in many parts of Ireland; its nest is always on the ground. In winter both are more widespread, and locally frequent in the south, but the goosander prefers fresh water, most notably the reservoirs of the Midlands and the London area, whereas the merganser stays mostly on salt water.

Both the larger sawbills somewhat resemble grebes or divers when swimming in the water, but their plumages are quite distinct. The two drakes are very striking, with their head and upper neck dark bottle-green, but the smaller merganser can be recognized by its chestnut breast-band and more prominent crest or mane. The ducks and immatures are even more alike, with chestnut-brown head and neck, the best distinction, when no drake is present, being the more sharply defined white patch on the chin.

Sawbills feed largely on fish and their fry, which is why the two larger ones have been deprived of protection in Scotland. Modern knowledge of the relations between predators and their prey suggests that this attitude towards the sawbills is ill-founded.

The GOLDENEYE (top) is a widespread winter visitor, more frequent than the goosander on fresh water in many parts of England. Individuals and pairs often stay so late into the spring that breeding is suspected, but this has never been proved in the British Isles, except perhaps in Cheshire in 1931 and 1932. It is another tree-nesting duck, in Scandinavia often using the old holes of the great black woodpecker, but though nest-boxes have been erected by Scottish lochs where goldeneyes linger late in spring, no pair has yet been tempted to use one. Goldeneyes are distinguished by their curiously shaped head, and the drake also by the prominent white spot on its dark bottle-green head. Ducks and immatures have chestnut-brown heads. Beware, incidentally, the old fowlers' use of the name goldeneye for the tufted duck.

The SMEW (bottom) is the smallest and least frequent of our three sawbills, and is in fact, after the teal, our second smallest wintering duck. It is not infrequent on reservoirs in Essex and the Thames valley, but elsewhere is rather scarce. The smew is one of the latest arrivals among our winter visitors, rarely seen before December and departing again in March. The drake in the black-and-white plumage known to fowlers as the 'white nun' is one of our most handsome wildfowl; the ducks and immatures are brown-headed, like the two larger sawbills.

ALL THREE

Family: Duck Family, Anatidae.
Males are Drakes, *Females* Ducks and
Young Ducklings.
Further Reading: *The Waterfowl of
the World.*
(See also under *Birds* on p. 95.)

GOOSANDER

Scientific Name: *Mergus merganser.*
Red-breasted Merganser, *M. serra-
tor.*
Length: 24–26 inches, drakes are
larger than ducks.
Habitat: Freshwater lakes, reservoirs
and rivers.
Breeding Season: April to June.
Protection: Throughout the year in
England and Wales; not protected
in Scotland.

GOLDENEYE

Scientific Name: *Bucephala clan-
gula.*
Length: 15–18 inches, drakes are
larger than ducks.
Habitat: Freshwater lakes and reservoirs, estuaries.
Protection: Throughout the year,
with special penalties from 1 February to 31 August.

SMEW

Scientific Name: *Mergus albellus.*
Length: 14–16 inches, drakes are
larger than ducks.
Habitat: Freshwater lakes and reser-
voirs, estuaries.
Protection: Throughout the year.

51

Lady Amherst's Pheasant : Reeves's Pheasant : Japanese Pheasant : Silver Pheasant

Besides those mentioned on page 54, four other pheasant species have been turned down in our woods and coverts from time to time. The only one that has firmly established itself, however, is LADY AMHERST'S PHEASANT (top left), which is so close a relative of the golden pheasant that the two almost invariably interbreed if they are turned down together. Its plumage is in some ways even more strikingly beautiful. Lady Amherst's comes from further west in China than the golden, its range extending from western Szechwan south to north-eastern Burma. In Britain at the present day it can be found in the woods of two districts: southern Bedfordshire, where it has spread from Woburn Park, and the New Forest, where it has escaped from Exbury. Nearly forty years ago an unsuccessful attempt was made to establish Lady Amherst's in Richmond Park, Surrey.

REEVES'S PHEASANT (bottom right) from northern China is one of the largest of all pheasants, the cock's tail sometimes attaining a length of six feet. It has been turned down at various times in several parts of Great Britain, but its reputation for driving other pheasants away makes it unpopular with keepers. Reeves's also interbreeds with common pheasants and has a tiresome tendency to wander far away from the estate where it was released. The first known wild breeding colony in Britain lived for several years at the end of the last century in Strathglass in western Inverness-shire, and there were some in Glen Urquhart at about the same time. These all apparently died out, but more recently some more have been turned down not very far away in Ross-shire; these birds are beginning to settle down, but it is too soon to say if the experiment will succeed. Although Reeves's pheasants have at various times been released in Bedfordshire, Gloucestershire, Kent, and several other counties in both England and Scotland, there is at present no fully established wild stock anywhere in the British Isles.

The JAPANESE PHEASANT (top right) has been introduced on a good many occasions since 1840, but has never established itself in the wild as a pure breeding population, although there were some very Japanese-like pheasants at large in the Sevenoaks district of Kent about twenty-five years ago. What the Japanese has done is to interbreed freely with its close relative the common pheasant, and there is every reason to suppose that it has played an important part in bringing the so-called melanistic mutant strain into our ordinary pheasant population. This strain has more than once turned up on an estate some years after the introduction of Japanese pheasants there, though it seems at present to be perpetuated largely by game farmers.

The handsome SILVER or KALIJ PHEASANT (bottom left) has often been turned down, but has never fully established itself anywhere in the wild for more than a few years. At present there are silver pheasants at large within the confines of both Woburn Park and Whipsnade Zoo in Bedfordshire, but they rarely venture outside.

ALL FOUR

Family: Pheasant Family, Phasiani-
dae.
Males are Cocks, *Females* Hens and
Young Chicks.
Habitat: Woodland and shrubberies
in parks and ornamental grounds.
Breeding Season: Spring.
Protection: Close season, 2 February
to 30 September.
Further Reading: *The Pheasants of
the World,* by Jean Delacour (1951);
The Ark in Our Midst.

LADY AMHERST'S
PHEASANT

Scientific Name: *Chrysolophus am-
herstiae.*
Length: Cocks 52–68 inches, Hens
c. 25 inches.

REEVES'S PHEASANT

Scientific Name: *Syrmaticus reevesi.*
Length: Cocks 48–84 inches, Hens
30–40 inches.

JAPANESE PHEASANT

Scientific Name: *Phasianus versi-
color.*
Length: Cocks 30–35 inches, Hens
21–25 inches.

SILVER PHEASANT

Scientific Name: *Lophura leuco-
melana.*
Length: Cocks *c.*40 inches; Hens *c.*20
inches.

Pheasant : Golden Pheasant

All too many books still repeat as if it were an established fact that the PHEASANT, an Asiatic bird, was introduced to Britain by the Romans. While this may be so, we have no evidence at all that there were in fact any pheasants in Roman Britain, nor even that they were known to the Saxons until a few years before the Norman Conquest. It is now more than thirty years since the late Dr Percy Lowe showed that the bones in Romano–British kitchen middens which were thought to be pheasants' did in fact belong to the domestic fowl, which in those days was a much scraggier bird than today's portly egg-machines.

The first solid evidence of pheasants in Britain comes from a bill of fare drawn up by Earl (later King) Harold for the monks of Waltham Abbey in Essex for the period between Michaelmas 1058 and Ash Wednesday 1059. This classed one pheasant as equivalent to two partridges. Pheasants may well have been one of the aspects of European civilization that the Normans brought to England, and at first they probably kept them in pens. Not till the turn of the twelfth century do we get any indication that there were wild pheasants in the woods, and throughout the Middle Ages they must have been scarce and local birds. There do not seem to have been any pheasants at all in Wales, Scotland or Ireland until Tudor days, and in some parts of those countries, as well as in the remoter north-western and south-western parts of England, such as Dartmoor, pheasants did not appear till about 150 years ago.

The first pheasants brought to Britain were of the dark-necked Caucasian race shown in the plate opposite, since erroneously dubbed the 'old English' pheasant. During the eighteenth century, however, many landowners augmented their dwindling stocks by large introductions of the ring-necked or Chinese pheasant, which has a white patch on either side of its neck. Since then pheasants of several other races have also been turned down in various parts of the country, so that our present stock is a complete amalgam, predominantly ring-necked but with many of the 'old English' type also.

The cock GOLDEN PHEASANT from central China is one of the most gorgeous of a family of many resplendent species. Landowners have therefore often turned it down as much to embellish their estates as to provide extra sport. Indeed the golden pheasant has a poor reputation among keepers, as an aggressive bird that tends to drive other pheasants away from their food. Its other drawback is its tendency to interbreed with its equally beautiful relative, Lady Amherst's pheasant (p. 52), so that the two cannot be released on the same estate.

Like many other introduced birds, the golden pheasant has been released in many more places than where it now survives. Today you are most likely to come across one in the Breckland of north-western Suffolk and south-western Norfolk, around Brandon and Thetford. They also exist in the woods in parts of Galloway, especially around the Duke of Bedford's estate at Cairnsmore, and in the Sevenoaks district of Kent.

BOTH PHEASANTS

Family: Pheasant Family, Phasianidae.

Males are Cocks, *Females* Hens and *Young* Chicks.

Breeding Season: April–May.

Protection: Close season, 2 February to 30 September.

Further Reading: *The Pheasants of the World*, by Jean Delacour (1951); *The Ark in Our Midst*.

PHEASANT

Scientific Name: *Phasianus colchicus.* 'Old English' Pheasant, *P. c. colchicus.* Chinese Ring-necked Pheasant, *P. c. torquatus.*

Length: Cocks 30–35 inches; Hens 21–25 inches.

Habitat: Woodland and farmland, also reed-beds.

GOLDEN PHEASANT

Scientific Name: *Chrysolophus pictus.*

Length: Cocks 40–44 inches; Hens *c.*25 inches.

Habitat: Woodland.

Red-legged Partridge : Rabbit

The RED-LEGGED or FRENCH PARTRIDGE is one of the most successful alien birds introduced into Britain. It is now common in many parts of eastern England, often outnumbering our native partridge, and is also more thinly distributed north to Yorkshire and west to Somerset. The first introductions, in the latter half of the seventeenth century, including one by King Charles II in Richmond Park and Windsor Great Park, all failed. Sporadic attempts continued until about 1790, when two noblemen with estates on the sandy soils near the Suffolk coast imported several thousand eggs from the Continent, and succeeded at once. They were followed by others, but it was from East Suffolk that the red-leg really set out to conquer England. Even as late as 1961 some were turned down in Perthshire, Scotland being at present outwith the bird's normal British range.

The red-legged partridge is a native of France south of the Loire and of the Iberian peninsula, and provides a remarkable example of a bird that has become thoroughly naturalized well to the north of its natural range. Those sportsmen who still like to walk their partridges up over dogs dislike the 'Frenchman', because it runs ahead instead of flying up like our native bird. At one time sportsmen of this persuasion were so prejudiced against the incomer that they would shoot it at any season, even on the nest! However, landowners who prefer to drive their partridges encourage the red-leg, which is so well suited to the lighter soils of eastern England.

Many people fail to realize that the RABBIT is not a native British animal at all, so familiar a part of our countryside was it up to the great myxomatosis epidemic of 1953–5. There is no evidence for the assertion, which is still sometimes made, that the rabbit was originally introduced by the Romans, and there now seems little doubt that the ancestors of our present stock did in fact arrive nearly a thousand years later. It is significant that Domesday Book, that comprehensive catalogue of English rural resources in the later eleventh century, says nothing about warrens. Yet just over a hundred years later we begin to hear of conies, as they were then called, and their warrens, jealously guarded properties yielding a highly prized meat. We know there were rabbits in the Isles of Scilly in 1176, and on Lundy in the Bristol Channel not very long afterwards. Just when they escaped from the warrens and began to spread over the countryside we do not know, but it could well have been during the period of labour shortage following the Black Death.

At all events, by the eighteenth century the rabbit was well distributed in the more cultivated parts of England, though still scarce or unknown in the wilder north and west, and in Wales, Scotland and Ireland. Its period of greatest abundance was the hundred years or so down to 1953. Many people feared that myxomatosis would completely exterminate the rabbit, but this has not happened, and a small, more or less immune population has survived and is slowly building up again, to the accompaniment of minor outbreaks of the disease. But it is still quite an event to see a rabbit in some parts of the country.

RED-LEGGED PARTRIDGE

Family: Pheasant Family, Phasiani-
dae.
Scientific Name: *Alectoris rufa*.
Males are Cocks, *Females* Hens and
Young Chicks.
Length: 13–14 inches.
Habitat: Farmland, mainly on light
soils.
Breeding Season: April to June.
Protection: Close season, 2 February
to 31 August.
Further Reading: *The Ark in Our
Midst.*

(See also under *Birds* on p. 95.)

RABBIT

Family: Hare Family, Leporidae.
Scientific Name: *Oryctolagus cuni-
culus*.
Males are Bucks, *Females* Does.
Length: 14–16 inches.
Habitat: Farmland, downland and
open country generally.
Breeding Season: Throughout the
year, but mainly from January to
June.
Protection: None; it is a scheduled
pest.
Further Reading: *The Rabbit*, by
Harry V. Thompson and Alastair
N. Worden (New Naturalist, 1956);
The Ark in Our Midst.

Little Tern : Roseate Tern : Black Tern : Gull-billed Tern

Two of these four terns are breeding species, the little tern widespread but decreasing, the roseate much more local. The black tern is a regular passage migrant, and only the fourth, the gull-billed tern, can properly be termed rare. All terns, of course, are summer visitors to the British Isles.

The LITTLE TERN (middle left) was once widespread on sandy and shingly beaches all round the British Isles, though always scarce in South Wales. Increasing pressure by holidaymakers and others has, however, severely affected its colonies on the beaches of eastern and southern England, so that in recent years it has become comparatively scarce in this region. In Hampshire the naturalists' trust takes special measures to protect one of the most vulnerable of these southern little terneries, but even so thoughtless yachtsmen and others are liable to land and picnic so close to it as to interfere with incubation. As its name suggests, the little tern is our smallest sea tern, easily distinguished from the others by its black-tipped yellow bill and white forehead. Its dainty flight as it dives into the water after sand-eels and other tiny fish adds greatly to the pleasure of a day by the sea, and it is sad that thoughtlessness by some holidaymakers should deprive others of this pleasure.

The ROSEATE TERN (bottom) is our least common breeding tern, being largely confined to Ireland, with about ten colonies, Anglesey, and a handful of spots on the east and south-west coasts of Scotland. Occasional pairs also breed in colonies of other terns in Norfolk, the Farne Islands (Northumberland), North-west England, Dorset and the Scilly Isles. The roseate differs from the common and arctic terns, both about the same size, in having a black bill, with a red base in summer, and a pink flush on its breast in spring. Experienced bird watchers can also pick the roseate out of a swirling flock of other terns by its distinctive call-note, a harsh, grating *aach, aach.*

The BLACK TERN (middle right), a marsh tern which breeds on fresh water, used to do so in eastern England until the middle of the last century, and still nests in Holland. The last definite breeding was on Romney Marsh, Kent about 1885, though a pair or two may have bred in Pett Level, not far away in Sussex, when it was flooded as part of our defences against invasion early in the Second World War. Today the black tern is a regular passage migrant, in spring and autumn, sometimes in flocks of a hundred or more, over lakes and reservoirs, mainly in the south-eastern half of England. Its striking summer plumage, grey with jet-black head and underparts, distinguishes it at once from all our other terns, except the rare white-winged black tern, whose white wings are distinctive at this time of year. In autumn and winter the general plumage pattern of the black tern is like that of the sea terns, grey with a black crown.

The GULL-BILLED TERN (top) is a rare visitor, though seen almost annually nowadays, that breeds just across the North Sea in Denmark, and did so on an Essex reservoir in 1949 and 1950.

58

ALL FOUR

Family: Gull Family, Laridae.
Scientific Names: Common Tern, *Sterna hirundo.* Arctic Tern, *S. paradisaea.* White-winged Black Tern, *Chlidonias leucopterus.*
Further Reading: *Sea Swallows,* by G. Marples (1934).
(See also under *Birds* on p. 95.)

LITTLE TERN

Scientific Name: *Sterna albifrons.*
Length: 9–10 inches.
Habitat: Shingly and sandy shores and marine islands.
Breeding Season: May to July.
Protection: Throughout the year.

ROSEATE TERN

Scientific Name: *Sterna dougallii.*
Length: 14–15 inches.
Habitat: Shingly and sandy shores and marine islands.
Breeding Season: June–July.
Protection: Throughout the year, with special penalties.

BLACK TERN

Scientific Name: *Chlidonias niger.*
Length: 9–10 inches.
Habitat: Reservoirs, broads and other fresh water, also estuaries.
Protection: Throughout the year, with special penalties.

GULL-BILLED TERN

Scientific Name: *Gelochelidon nilotica.*
Length: 14–15 inches.
Habitat: Coastal.
Protection: Throughout the year.

Spoonbill : Bittern

Though a few SPOONBILLS come to Britain across the North Sea every year, on migration to and from their breeding places in the Netherlands, they are only likely to be seen by lucky watchers on east- and south-coast estuaries. Breydon Water on the borders of Norfolk and Suffolk is the most likely single spot to see one. A handful may also spend the winter in Devon or Cornwall.

Few people realize that the spoonbill once nested in England. Our knowledge that it did so quite close to London we owe to the litigiousness of a former Bishop of London, who in 1523 sued a citizen to whom he had leased part of his park at Fulham, to restrain him from taking herons and 'shovelers', as spoonbills were then called, from their nests in the trees in the park. Old records also show that spoonbills bred in Sussex during the reign of Queen Elizabeth I, and in East Anglia in the middle of the following century. Today the Dutch colonies are the nearest ones to our shores, and there are no others nearer than Austria and southern Spain.

The spoonbill looks like an all-white heron, but is readily distinguished by its broad-tipped bill. At close quarters adult birds can be seen to have a yellowish breast-band and in summer also a yellowish crest. Immatures have the extreme tips of their wings blackish.

The BITTERN is one of that select group of four marsh birds which were lost as British breeding species in the last century, but have returned under careful protection in the present one; the others are the avocet (p. 64), black-tailed godwit and marsh harrier. Once so common among the fens and broads of East Anglia that in the 1820s four or five might be seen in a morning in the extensive reed-beds around Hickling and Potter Heigham in Norfolk, by 1850 the bittern had become extinct save as an occasional winter visitor. Only once in the next sixty years was a pair proved to breed, at Sutton in the Norfolk Broads in 1886, though doubtless a pair or two nested unobserved.

From 1900 onwards, however, bitterns were heard booming almost every spring in their favourite Norfolk Broads area, and in 1911 Miss E. L. Turner and Jim Vincent, Lord Desborough's keeper at Hickling, managed to find a single young bird in a dense swamp. From then onwards bitterns have not only nested annually in this area, but have spread to the coastal marshes of Suffolk and North Norfolk, and beyond to Cambridge-shire, Lincolnshire, Hampshire, Kent, North Lancashire and North Wales.

The bittern is one of our shyest birds, much preferring to stay in the shelter of dense reed-beds, when its presence can only be detected by its characteristic booming call, like the distant lowing of a cow. When it does choose to come out into the open, its hunched posture usually makes it look more like a brown goose than the brown heron it really is. When disturbed in the reeds, it may either freeze in an extraordinary attenu-ated upright posture, or take flight, when its broad rounded wings are distinctive.

SPOONBILL

Family: Ibis Family, Threskiorni-
thidae.
Scientific Name: *Platalea leucorodia.*
Length: 33–35 inches.
Habitat: Coastal marshes and estua-
ries.
Breeding Season: Has not bred in
Britain since the seventeenth cen-
tury.
Protection: Throughout the year,
with special penalties.
Further Reading: See under *Birds*
on p. 95.

BITTERN

Family: Heron Family, Ardeidae.
Scientific Name: *Botaurus stellaris.*
Length: 29–31 inches.
Habitat: Reed-beds, swamps and
marshes.
Breeding Season: April to June.
Protection: Throughout the year,
with special penalties.
Further Reading: *The Return of the
Osprey* (Chapter 6).
(See also under *Birds* on p. 95.)

61

Ruff : Bearded Tit

The RUFF is one of the three lost marshland birds which, unlike the bittern (p. 60) and the avocet (p. 64), have not yet firmly re-established themselves as breeding species in Britain; the other two are the black tern (p. 58) and Savi's warbler. The ruff hung on longer than any of the others, for it nested regularly, at least in Norfolk, till 1871, and sporadically on some ten other occasions in the eastern or north-eastern counties down to 1922, when the late Arnold Boyd found the last known British nest at Cley-next-the-Sea in North Norfolk. The end of the ruff has been a sad tale of persecution and cupidity by the collectors of birds' eggs and skins; in 1871, for instance, the whole progeny of two pairs which bred at Hickling, the last of the original stock of the Norfolk ruffs, was shot.

Today the ruff is a regular passage migrant, not infrequent in some districts, being most often seen on the east and south coasts between the Firth of Forth and Dorset; a few sometimes stay the winter. In spring it is one of our earliest migrants, often appearing in force in March. Most of these birds are probably on their way to or from their breeding grounds in Norway and the Netherlands.

The most remarkable feature of the ruff is the extraordinary headgear of the male in breeding plumage, consisting of a ruff and ear-tufts that may be almost any combination of black, brown, buff or white, either plain, streaked or barred, and with the ruff usually coloured differently from the ear-tufts. Both reeves and winter ruffs look rather like redshanks, but with highly variable bill and leg colour, the bill red, yellow or brown, and the legs green, yellow, orange, or flesh-coloured, and of course without the conspicuous white of the redshank's wings. Ruffs and reeves also take part in communal courtship ceremonies at special display grounds known as 'hills'.

Not so long ago the BEARDED TIT was definitely a rare bird, but nowadays scarce or local would be more appropriate terms. The bearded tit never went right under like the ruff and six other marshland birds, but it did become virtually restricted to the Norfolk Broads. During the past thirty years, however, it has increased under careful protection and has spread to other parts of East Anglia, notably the coastal marshes of Suffolk and North Norfolk, and the population has built up so much that since about 1960 there have been regular mass emigrations from its breeding grounds to reed-beds further west. The birds have actually been watched departing, especially from the Minsmere reserve of the Royal Society for the Protection of Birds on the Suffolk coast. In 1965 they travelled for greater distances and in greater numbers than ever before, and reached Devon, Cornwall, the Scilly Isles, Somerset, Glamorgan, Anglesey, North Lancashire and Northumberland.

The bearded tit's long tail has earned it the local name of reed pheasant, and it is in fact the only small, long-tailed bird that is likely to be found in the reed-beds in which it spends its whole life. It is not now regarded as being in any way related to our garden tits.

RUFF

Family: Sandpiper Family, Scolopacidae.
Scientific Name: *Philomachus pugnax.*
Males are Ruffs, *Females* Reeves.
Length: 9–12 inches, ruffs are larger than reeves.
Habitat: Marshes and freshwater margins, also sometimes by the sea.
Breeding Season: Formerly May–June.
Protection: Throughout the year, with special penalties.
Further Reading: See under *Birds* on page 95.

BEARDED TIT

Family: Flycatcher Family, Muscicapidae.
Scientific Name: *Panurus biarmicus.*
Length: 6–7 inches.
Habitat: Extensive reed and sedge beds.
Breeding Season: April to July.
Protection: Throughout the year, with special penalties.
Further Reading: See under *Birds* on p. 95.

Avocet : Swallow-tail Butterfly

The return of the AVOCET to breed regularly in eastern England is the greatest achievement in the eighty years' history of the Royal Society for the Protection of Birds. The avocet thus joins the select group of marshland birds (see p. 62) which have succeeded in recolonizing Britain during the past sixty years. It was as long ago as 1824 that avocets ceased to breed in East Anglia, though they lingered in Lincolnshire till 1837 and in Kent till about 1843. The next certain breeding record in the British Isles was in 1938, when two pairs astoundingly turned up in Co. Wexford in the extreme south-eastern corner of Ireland, and nested there. Wartime activities soon afterwards evidently disturbed the avocet breeding colonies just across the North Sea in Holland, for a pair may have nested in North Norfolk in 1941, and one certainly did in Essex in 1944. This was a period when to be seen with a pair of binoculars on the east coast was to risk being bundled immediately off to a guard room, so other pairs may well have nested unobserved.

In 1946 another pair nested in North Norfolk, but the eggs are believed to have been stolen by a collector. In the following year four pairs bred in each of two spots on the Suffolk coast that were later to become famous as the star reserves of the R.S.P.B., Minsmere and Havergate Island. The Minsmere colony did not last, but avocets have nested at Havergate every year since, carefully guarded by the R.S.P.B.; in 1965 there were about fifty-two pairs. Curiously enough, avocets returned to breed at Minsmere again in 1965.

Even if it were not rare, the avocet would be worth going a long way to see, for it is one of our most strikingly attractive waders, with its black-and-white plumage and long curved bill. After the breeding season the birds scatter and are then likely to be seen on other parts of the east coast, while for some years a few have been wintering on estuaries in the south-west. It is not known whether these come from Suffolk or from Holland, but the chances are that they belong to the Havergate breeding stock.

The magnificent SWALLOW-TAIL BUTTERFLY is one of the most handsome as well as the largest and one of the rarest of our native butterflies. Formerly more widespread, it is now confined to the Norfolk Broads, where its caterpillars feed on the scarce milk parsley. For many years it was also one of the glories of Wicken Fen, the famous National Trust nature reserve in Cambridgeshire, but became extinct some years ago. Recent attempts to reintroduce it have not yet met with success. The swallow-tails of eastern England belong to a distinct British race, whereas those that occasionally turn up in Kent and other parts of southern England are of the Continental race, whose caterpillars are willing to eat other umbelliferous plants, such as wild angelica, fennel and wild carrot. There is some suggestion that at least in Kent these immigrants from Europe may sometimes breed for a year or two.

AVOCET

Family: Avocet Family, Recurvirostridae.

Scientific Name: *Recurvirostra avosetta*.

Length: 17 inches.

Habitat: Estuaries and brackish lagoons.

Breeding Season: April–July.

Migration: Late March to early October.

Protection: Throughout the year, with special penalties.

Further Reading: *The Return of the Osprey* (Chapters 3 and 4). (See also under *Birds* on p. 95.)

SWALLOW-TAIL BUTTERFLY

Family: Swallow-tail Family, Papilionidae.

Scientific Name: *Papilio machaon*. British Swallow-tail, *P. m. britannicus*. Continental Swallow-tail, *P. m. gorganus*.

Wing-span: *c*.3 inches, females are larger than males.

Habitat: Fens, broads and marshes in East Anglia; open country elsewhere.

On the Wing: May–June, occasionally August.

Food-plant: Milk Parsley, *Peucedanum palustre*.

Protection: None, except in nature reserves.

Further Reading: See under *Butterflies* on p. 95.

65

5

Golden Oriole : Purple Emperor

The cock GOLDEN ORIOLE is one of the most gorgeous of the rarities that visit the British Isles from time to time. Its bright yellow plumage with black wings is most striking on the comparatively rare occasions when the bird shows itself in full view. For it is a great skulker, and is more often heard than seen, uttering a loud, clear, musical *weela-weeo* note at frequent intervals. The yellowish-green hens are much less conspicuous than their resplendent mates.

A few orioles stray across the Channel or the North Sea almost every spring, and are perhaps most often seen near the coast in Kent or East Anglia, though Devon is another favoured county. Very occasionally a pair stays to nest, most often in Kent, but also at times in Norfolk, Suffolk, Devon, the Isle of Wight and other southern counties of England. To Wales, Scotland and Ireland the golden oriole is a distinctly rare visitor.

On the Continent, where it is frequent right along the Channel coast, except in Brittany and parts of Normandy, it can be found in well-timbered parks, large gardens, small plantations and copses, rather than extensive woodlands, while groves of evergreen or holm oaks are especially favoured. Here it builds its curious nest, slung like a hammock from two boughs of a tree, and towards the end of May or early in June lays its three or four purple-spotted white eggs.

The PURPLE EMPEROR is one of our handsomest butterflies, and also one of the most elusive. Not only is it very local in distribution, but its habits mean that only the early riser is likely to see it at close quarters, unless some carrion has appeared in its haunts, by accident or design. Professor Ford tells us that early in the morning it will descend from the trees and skim swiftly along the paths through one of its favourite oakwoods or beechwoods, but that long before midday it retreats to the summits again. Here it may be seen flying round, soaring high in the air or resting on the tips of the branches, well out of the reach of the lepidopterist's net. The lie-abed butterfly hunter, whom we may charitably suppose to have been up late the previous night catching moths, must resort to guile if he wishes to have a closer view. (In parenthesis, may it be said that one hopes that nowadays he will not wish to capture and kill this rare and beautiful insect, but will seek his specimens by rearing its caterpillars.) For the emperor has a weakness, which is his love of carrion. He may be seen sampling the wares at a keeper's gibbet, resting on the corpse of a dead rabbit on the ground, or even drinking from a foul-smelling puddle. Sometimes he also drinks the sap from an open wound in a tree.

To see the purple emperor nowadays, it is necessary to visit certain woods in Sussex, Northamptonshire and other southern and midland counties of England, whose detailed localities are kept secret by lovers of the butterfly, though it must be admitted that in some cases the secret is a fairly open one.

GOLDEN ORIOLE

Family: Oriole Family, Oriolidae.
Scientific Name: *Oriolus oriolus.*
Males are Cocks, *Females* Hens.
Length: 9–10 inches.
Habitat: Well-timbered parks and large gardens, copses and plantations.
Breeding Season: May–June.
Protection: Throughout the season, with special penalties.
Further Reading: See under *Birds* on p. 95.

PURPLE EMPEROR

Family: Peacock Family, Nymphalidae.
Scientific Name: *Apatura iris.*
Wing-span: 3 inches, females rather larger than males.
Habitat: Extensive oakwoods and sometimes beechwoods.
On the Wing: July–August.
Food-plant: Sallows, *Salix caprea* and *S. cinerea.*
Protection: Only in certain nature reserves.
Further Reading: See under *Butterflies* on p. 95.

67

Hobby : Long-tailed Blue

The HOBBY, whose curious name derives from the Old French word *hobé*, is a regular summer visitor to Britain, and one of the latest to arrive, rarely being seen before mid-May. Its aerial outline of long, scythe-shaped wings and rather short tail gives it the appearance of a small peregrine falcon or a giant swift, and its characteristic fast, dashing flight is often interrupted by a glide. Being so agile on the wing, it can capture and eat those others masters of the air, swallows and martins, whose migrating flocks the hobby sometimes follows.

The hobby is one of our rarer breeding birds of prey, with probably fewer than a hundred pairs nesting in southern and midland England each year. It has nested in the North of England, but is virtually unknown in the rest of the British Isles. Its strongholds are the mid-southern counties of Hampshire, Dorset and Wiltshire, with smaller numbers in Berkshire, Surrey and Sussex. North of the Thames it is rare, and breeds regularly only in the counties of Buckingham, Oxford, Gloucester, Hereford and Salop. In the rest of the Midlands and in East Anglia the hobby breeds only sporadically, while the past breeding records in Cheshire, Yorkshire and Wales were quite exceptional.

The type of country favoured by the hobby is rather hard to define, but usually includes scattered trees or belts of trees, and may comprise downland, farmland, heathland or open woodland. Its most favoured habitat in England seems to be the open downland of Wessex, with its shelter-belts of pine. The nest, always high up in a tree, often a pine or other conifer, is invariably the old nest of a carrion crow or some other bird, or even a squirrel's drey.

The LONG-TAILED BLUE, a native of southern Europe, is one of the rarest of the occasional butterfly migrants to Britain. It has occurred, almost always in southern England, on only about thirty occasions, the first being on 4 August 1859, near Christchurch, Hants. On the same day another was captured on the downs near Brighton, by a fortunate lepidopterist who caught a third in the same place on the following day. Only very rarely has the long-tailed blue successfully bred in England, its food plants being various members of the pea family, and it could never maintain itself through our cold, wet winters.

The rarest of all our rare blue butterflies is the short-tailed blue, of which only four specimens were caught between 1874 and 1945. Although it has never been known to breed in Britain, Professor Ford of the University of Oxford believes that it is not impossible that a few colonies may exist undetected in southern England. The short-tailed blue breeds as near our shores as Brittany, and is so remarkably similar to the silver-studded blue that it could easily be overlooked.

A third rare blue, the mazarine blue, did at one time apparently breed regularly here, at least in Dorset and Glamorgan, but became extinct before the end of the last century, and is now one of our rarest visitors.

HOBBY

Family: Falcon Family, Falconidae.
Scientific Name: *Falco subbuteo*.
Length: 12–14 inches, females usually larger than males.
Habitat: Downland and other types of country with scattered trees.
Migration: Arrives mid and late May; departs late September and early October.
Breeding Season: June–July.
Protection: Throughout the year, with special penalties.
Further Reading: See under *Birds* on p. 95.

LONG-TAILED BLUE

Family: Copper Family, Lycaenidae.
Scientific Name: *Lampides boeticus*.
Short-tailed Blue, *Everes argiades*.
Mazarine Blue, *Cyaniris semiargus*.
Wing-span: $1\frac{1}{4}$ inches.
Habitat: Gardens and rough grassy places.
On the Wing: July to September.
Food-plants: Pea Family, Leguminosae.
Further Reading: See under *Butterflies on* p. 95.

Yellow Wagtails : Monarch Butterfly

The YELLOW WAGTAIL (centre) is one of the few birds that are virtually confined to the British Isles, but has no claim to be considered rare, except in Scotland, where it breeds regularly only in the Clyde area, and in Ireland, where it has recently become extinct. A locally frequent summer visitor, arriving early in April and staying until September, it has two quite distinct types of habitat, marshes and damp grassland on the one hand, and dry heaths, moors and farmland on the other. The yellow wagtail is not especially associated with streams and running water, a habitat most favoured by the Grey Wagtail, a bird with which the yellow wagtail is all too often confused by the uninitiated, both species having both grey and yellow in their plumage. The two are best separated by the larger size, longer tail and grey upperparts of the grey wagtail, whose cock also sports a black gorget in its summer plumage. The cock yellow wagtail, on the other hand, is one of the most brilliantly yellow of all British birds. Any grey and yellow wagtail seen by fresh water between mid-October and mid-March can be confidently set down as a grey wagtail.

The BLUE-HEADED WAGTAIL (top) is the race of the yellow wagtail (or more strictly and less insularly the yellow wagtail is a race of the blue-headed wagtail) which breeds over the greater part of Europe; it occurs as a scarce migrant mainly on the east side of Great Britain, and has nested a few times. The GREY-HEADED WAGTAIL (bottom) is the race of the blue-headed/yellow wagtail that breeds in northern Scandinavia, and occurs sparingly in Britain on migration, mainly in the Scottish isles. Two other races of this wagtail have occurred here very rarely: the black-headed wagtail from the Balkans and the ashy-headed wagtail from the Mediterranean.

The handsome MONARCH or MILKWEED BUTTERFLY, the largest butterfly that ever occurs wild in the British Isles, is a rarity that is one of the great prizes of the butterfly enthusiast. A native of North America, it is noted for its long-distance migrations. Each year thousands of monarchs spend the winter in semi-hibernation in clusters in the southern United States, mainly Florida and California. In the spring they migrate northwards, breeding as they go on their food-plant, the American milkweed *Asclepias*, until they reach Canada, whence they or their descendants return southwards in the autumn.

Within recent years the monarch has not only crossed the Atlantic, establishing a breeding colony on the Canary Islands *en route*, but has spread across the Pacific to Australia and the East Indies. Professor E. B. Ford has made out a strong case that despite the monarch's known ability to fly long distances, most of these transatlantic journeys have in fact been made on board ship. Numbers of monarchs have, for instance, been seen flying round the potato locker of a ship just before a transatlantic voyage, and there are similar indications. The American milkweeds, which are quite different from the European plants of the same name, are too tender to grow in Britain, so no breeding colony is ever likely to result from the occasional transatlantic visitors, whether they come by sea or on their own wings.

YELLOW WAGTAILS

Family: Wagtail Family, Motacillidae.

Scientific Names: Yellow Wagtail, *Motacilla flava flavissima*. Blue-headed Wagtail, *M. f. flava*. Grey-headed Wagtail, *M. f. thunbergi*. Black-headed Wagtail, *M. f. feldegg*. Ashy-headed Wagtail, *M. f. cinereocapilla*. Grey Wagtail, *M. cinerea*. *Males* are Cocks, *Females* Hens.

Length: 6½ inches.

Habitat: Marshes, damp grassland, heaths and farmland.

Breeding Season: May to July.

Protection: Throughout the year.

Further Reading: *The Yellow Wagtail,* by Stuart Smith (New Naturalist, 1950).

(See also under *Birds* on p. 95.)

MONARCH BUTTERFLY

Family: Monarch Family, Danaidae.

Scientific Name: *Danaus plexippus*.

Wing-span: 4 inches.

On the Wing: June to October.

Protection: None.

Further Reading: See under *Butterflies* on p. 95.

Hoopoe : Dormouse

When it is at rest, the most conspicuous feature of the handsome and striking HOOPOE is its crest, which may or may not be raised, but in flight its black-and-white wing pattern at once shows up, and with its rounded wings the bird looks like nothing so much as a giant pied moth. The hoopoe is an annual visitor to the British Isles in small numbers, especially in spring. It is sufficiently numerous not to be considered a rare bird for the purposes of the Rarities Committee of the journal *British Birds,* but nevertheless any British bird-watcher is well pleased with himself if he succeeds in seeing one on his native heath, and there are only a very few places, such as the Scilly Isles, where one can confidently be expected in the course of a year. Just across the Channel, of course, it is another matter, for hoopoes breed regularly throughout France right up to the shores of La Manche.

From time to time the hoopoe has actually nested within the Four Seas, its nest always being in a hole in a tree or wall. It used to be said that if only collectors would refrain from shooting it in the spring, the hoopoe would colonize at any rate southern England and breed here regularly. However, it must now be a good many years since a skin collector shot a hoopoe for his private collection in Britain, and though a few doubtless fall victim each year to those mindless louts who kill everything that flies, this is clearly not the factor that has hitherto prevented the hoopoe from establishing itself in Britain. More probably our climate is to blame, and perhaps also the absence of the right kind of insect food.

The DORMOUSE is much scarcer today than it was fifty or sixty years ago. Even then it was common only in the south of England, being less frequent in the west and north, and distinctly uncommon in the Midlands and East Anglia. In Scotland and Ireland it was, and is, unknown. At one time the dormouse was commonly kept as a pet, and partly as a result of this, several attempts have been made to introduce it in parts of the country where it was scarce or unknown. All attempts failed, but an introduced colony did survive in Norfolk for at least thirty-five years.

Its association with the Mad Hatter's tea party is not the only remarkable fact about the dormouse. It is our only native mouse-like rodent with a bushy tail. It is the only British mammal that genuinely hibernates, becoming completely torpid and lying up just below the ground. This is the period when it is most vulnerable to predators, being preyed on while it is helpless not only by crows and magpies but probably also by badgers, foxes and stoats. The dormouse is strictly nocturnal, sleeping singly during the day in specially constructed nests woven out of dried grass or strips of honeysuckle bark.

The dormouse is also purely vegetarian, feeding on the fruits, shoots and bark of trees and shrubs, such as hazel, beech and pine. Though in some parts of the Continent foresters regard it as a pest on account of damage to shoots in young plantations, there is no evidence whatever that this happens in Britain. There are far too few of this attractive little beast to make it other than a most welcome member to our somewhat exiguous mammal fauna.

HOOPOE

Family: Hoopoe Family, Upupidae.
Scientific Name: *Upupa epops.*
Length: 11–12 inches.
Habitat: Parks, large gardens and other areas with scattered timber; often feeds on lawns.
Breeding Season: May–June.
Protection: Throughout the year, with special penalties.
Further Reading: See under *Birds* on p. 95.

DORMOUSE

Family: Dormouse Family, Gliridae.
Scientific Name: *Muscardinus avellanarius.*
Length: 6–7 inches.
Breeding Season: June to September.
Protection: None.
Further Reading: See under *Mammals* on p. 95.

73

Serin : Edible Dormouse

The SERIN is a small greenish-yellow finch, closely related to the domesticated canary, which is descended from a form of serin inhabiting the Canary Islands, the Azores and Madeira. It is even smaller than a siskin, from which it differs in having a more prominent yellow rump but no yellow at the base of the tail, and is substantially smaller than a greenfinch.

The serin is not migratory, but over the past hundred years or so it has been advancing steadily northwards on the Continent, and now breeds commonly just across the Channel in northern France. As long ago as 1926 E. M. Nicholson, later to become an outstanding director-general of the Nature Conservancy, prophesied that it would eventually establish itself as a breeding bird in Britain. This forecast, entirely reasonable at the time, has yet to be fulfilled, although in the intervening years the black redstart (p. 80), the collared dove (p. 80) and the little ringed plover have all arrived and established themselves.

It is only very recently that the serin has been recorded in Britain more than once or twice every few years. In 1958 and 1963, for instance, none at all were seen, and only one bird in each of 1959 and 1960, although in 1961, 1962 and 1964 there were five in each year. Eleven of these birds were seen, as one might expect, in the south-coast counties from Kent to the Scilly Isles, but others appeared as far north as Yorkshire and Lincolnshire, and as far west as Co. Cork in south-west Ireland. The serin is an inconspicuous little bird, and could easily be overlooked by people unfamiliar with its curious little whispering jingle of a song. It should, however, be looked or listened for in towns and villages along the south coast.

The EDIBLE DORMOUSE from Central Europe is a good deal larger than our native dormouse (p. 72), and is indeed more likely to be confused with a young grey squirrel (p. 18). It owes its name to the fact that it was highly regarded by Roman gourmets, who used to fatten it up for the table. In Britain it is one of the most localized of our established introduced aliens. Originally released by Lord Rothschild at Tring Park in Hertfordshire in 1902, it has since spread over an area of some hundred square miles in the Chilterns, roughly represented by the triangle Luton–Aylesbury–Beaconsfield, but no further. There seems to be no reason why it should not occupy at least the remainder of the Chilterns, but in recent years it has shown no signs of doing so, nor has anybody been able to offer a satisfactory explanation. It may well be partly due to the fact that the climate of the Chilterns is slightly more Continental than most of the surrounding areas.

Although a comparatively harmless animal—only one recent instance of damage to farming or forestry is known in Britain—it makes itself unpopular by coming indoors in the autumn to hibernate, and then is liable to make a noise in the rafters compared by one sufferer to 'a herd of small elephants'. The rodent control department at Amersham, Buckinghamshire, is said to receive regular complaints from householders whose slumbers have been disturbed by these antics.

SERIN

Family: Finch Family, Fringillidae.
Scientific Name: *Serinus serinus.*
Males are Cocks, *Females* Hens.
Length: 4½ inches.
Habitat: Well-timbered parks and
  gardens in towns, suburbs and
  villages.
Breeding Season: Has not yet bred
  in Britain.
Protection: Throughout the year.
Further Reading: See under *Birds*
  on p. 95.

EDIBLE DORMOUSE

Family: Dormouse Family, Gliridae.
Scientific Name: *Glis glis.*
Length: 13–15 inches.
Breeding Season: June to August.
Protection: None.
Further Reading: *The Ark in Our
  Midst.*
(See also under *Mammals* on p. 95.)

Bee-eater : Rosy Starling

The BEE-EATER's brilliant harlequin attire makes it perhaps the most gorgeous of all our bird rarities. It earns its name by indeed eating bees, wasps and similar winged insects, and has a graceful swallow-like flight, with long glides on level, triangular wings. When on the wing, it constantly utters a liquid cry, *quilp, quilp*. Like the kingfisher and the sand martin, its nest is always made in a hole in a sandy or gravelly bank.

A few bee-eaters are seen almost every year somewhere in the southern counties of England, occasionally penetrating to the north of Scotland and the west of Ireland. Though it is normally a highly gregarious bird, these lost stragglers in Britain are often solitary. A Mediterranean, North African and western Asiatic bird in origin, it does not normally breed nearer to the British Isles than northern Spain and southern France, but in 1955 three pairs nested in a sand-pit in Sussex, where they were seen by hundreds of bird-watchers from all over the country, while in 1920 a pair attempted to breed as far north as Edinburgh. In winter the European bee-eater migrates southwards into Africa, where it may be seen alongside several other equally brightly coloured species.

Only one other kind of bee-eater has been recorded in the British Isles. A single specimen of the blue-cheeked bee-eater from North Africa was seen on St Agnes in the Isles of Scilly on 22 June 1951.

The ROSY STARLING, rosy pastor or rose-coloured starling, is, as its name suggests, a relative of our common starling, and indeed young birds are hard to pick out in a flock of young starlings, although their plumage is still paler. The adults, resplendent in pink and black, are unmistakable.

A handful of rosy starlings are reported from some part of the British Isles every year, but as this is a popular cage-bird, it is impossible to be sure that they have all arrived unaided from their native haunts in eastern Europe, the south Russian steppes and Persia. It is usually considered that birds seen in the Shetlands, or at the nearby Fair Isle Bird Observatory, where one or two appear in most years, must be genuinely wild, but there can be no real certainty, for escaped cage-birds have more than once wandered as far north as this. The rosy starling has never been known to breed in the British Isles.

The rosy starling is omnivorous, like our native starling, but in parts of its range it feeds to a large extent on grasshoppers and locusts, whose swarms it follows. Indeed in the Crimea the arrival of rosy starlings is held to foretell the appearance of swarms of locusts. Dr Bannerman tells us that both the Armenians and the Tartars treat the rosy starling as a sacred bird because of its value in controlling locusts, despite the fact that at other times it is liable to ravage their crops of cherries and mulberries.

76

BEE-EATER

Family: Bee-eater Family, Meropi-
dae.
Scientific Name: *Merops apiaster*.
Blue-cheeked Bee-eater, *M. super-
ciliosus*.
Length: 11 inches.
Habitat: No special preference in
Britain, but nests in sandy banks.
Breeding Season: June.
Protection: Throughout the year,
with special penalties.
Further Reading: See under *Birds*
on p. 95.

ROSY STARLING

Family: Starling Family, Sturnidae.
Scientific Name: *Pastor roseus*.
Length: 8–9 inches.
Habitat: In Britain often accom-
panies flocks of starlings.
Breeding Season: Has never bred in
Britain.
Protection: Throughout the year.
Further Reading: See under *Birds*
on p. 95.

Waxwing : Snow Bunting

The WAXWING, a circumpolar species whose range extends from Lapland eastabout to western Arctic Canada, is the classic example of an irregular winter visitor to the British Isles. In some winters none at all, or just a handful, are seen, but in others the waxwing is widespread and comparatively frequent throughout the greater part of Britain. Usually these 'waxwing years' are fairly widely separated, but occasionally, as in 1956–60, they occur for several years running. Most of our birds probably come from Lapland and Finland.

One of the attractive features of the waxwing for the rare bird fancier is that in a waxwing year he need not go to a sewage farm or some remote windswept estuary to see it, for it is most often seen on the berry-bearing shrubs of parks and gardens, such as pyracantha, cotoneaster, holly, berberis, hawthorn and rowan or mountain ash. Indeed it is now generally agreed that it is the failure of the rowan crop in northern Scandinavia that usually triggers off the invasions or irruptions of the waxwing. Crossbills (p. 28) are subject to similar movements when the spruce crop fails.

Waxwings, called Bohemian chatterers by the older writers and Bohemian waxwings in North America, derive their name from the curious red patches on the tips of their wing feathers, which look remarkably like sealing wax. Its crest usually enables the bird to be picked out in poor light or other conditions when its distinctive yellow tail-tip and red-and-yellow wing patches cannot be seen clearly.

The SNOW BUNTING is rare only as a breeding species. As a winter visitor it is fairly frequent on parts of the east coast, but less so on other coasts. It also occurs inland on hills, for instance in the Scottish Highlands and the Lancashire Pennines. A flock of snow buntings in flight, flashing white in the sun, is a most attractive sight, and the birds have been well named 'snowflakes'. Flocks of snow buntings can be extraordinarily faithful to their wintering grounds; one flock, for instance, frequented Arthur's Seat at Edinburgh for many years. Murrayfield, the rugby football ground at Edinburgh, is another favoured haunt, where the birds can even be seen flying round while a match is in progress.

As a breeding species in Scotland the snow bunting, another circumpolar bird, reaches almost its southernmost point in the Old World. Only in Kamchatka, the Aleutians and Labrador does it come further south. It is doubtful if the snow bunting breeds regularly on any Scottish mountain, but it is most frequent on the Cairngorms and some of the Sutherland hills. Desmond Nethersole-Thompson, whose knowledge of the rarer Highland breeding birds is extensive, believes that breeding only takes place if a pair or small group of snow buntings happens to stay behind out of a wintering flock. These continue to breed for several years until a hard winter or some other factor wipes out the small population. Evidently the Highlands are a highly marginal breeding territory for the snow bunting.

WAXWING

Family: Waxwing Family, Bombycillidae.

Scientific Name: *Bombycilla garrulus*.

Length: 7 inches.

Habitat: Parks, gardens, scrub and other places with berry-bearing scrubs.

Protection: Throughout the year.

Further Reading: See under *Birds* on p. 95.

SNOW BUNTING

Family: Finch Family, Fringillidae.

Scientific Name: *Plectrophenax nivalis*.

Males are Cocks, *Females* Hens.

Length: 6½ inches.

Habitat: Mountain tops in summer; mountains, high moors and sea shores in winter.

Breeding Season: May to July.

Protection: Throughout the year, with special penalties.

Further Reading: See under *Birds* on p. 95.

79

Collared Dove : Black Redstart

The COLLARED DOVE is the latest arrival among the half-dozen birds which have colonized Britain by natural means during the present century, never having bred here before. In size it is intermediate between the woodpigeon and the turtle dove, differing from both in having a black half-collar on each side of its neck. Its call-note, soon likely to be as familiar to Britons as the woodpigeon's coo, is a triple *du-duu-duh*.

No other bird is known ever to have colonized so much new territory so rapidly as the collared dove in its headlong advance north-westwards across central and western Europe during the past thirty-five years. Starting from the Danube valley around Belgrade about 1930, its rapid spread had carried it across the North Sea by 1955, or perhaps even by 1952, when a single bird (which the pundits still insist might have escaped from a cage somewhere) appeared in Lincolnshire. It was not until 1956 that the first pairs were actually proved to breed, in North Norfolk, not far from Cromer, and having got this toehold in Britain the collared dove has never looked back. Even in 1957 it had already reached the shores of the Moray Firth, and by 1964 it had colonized the greater part of England, Wales and Scotland and was already making inroads on Ireland.

The secret of the collared dove's success is its ability to pick up a living from the grain scattered, by accident or design, in chicken-runs and farmyards. Already saturation point has been reached in some districts, and it has been forecast that within ten years or so there will be collared doves in every town, suburb and village in the British Isles, just as there are blackbirds and robins today. This prophecy is all too likely to be fulfilled.

The BLACK REDSTART has also spread north-westwards across Europe, but more slowly, over a period of nearly 200 years. It is a robin-like little bird, whose cock differs from its close relative, the cock common redstart, in its plumage being all black, except for a white wing-patch and the rufous tail. The hen is much browner, but still has the rufous tail. It is a not infrequent passage migrant, mainly on the coast, and occasionally stays the winter in the south-west.

The continuous history of the black redstart as a breeding bird in Britain starts in 1923, when a nest was found on the Sussex cliffs near Hastings, but only a handful of pairs nested in any year up to the war. The bombing of London and coastal towns in the south-east during the 1940s produced a rubbly habitat admirably suited to this originally mountain bird, and the known number of breeding pairs rose steadily, till in 1950 they reached an all-time high of thirty-eight, all in the south-eastern half of England. Then numbers fell, until in the early 1960s there were fewer than fifteen known pairs. For twenty years the bombed sites of London and Dover were the two main breeding haunts of the black redstart, but by 1966 these were almost all rebuilt, so that other south-east coastal towns, mainly between Yarmouth and Eastbourne, together with the more industrialized suburbs of London are now its main strongholds.

COLLARED DOVE

Family: Dove Family, Columbidae.
Scientific Name: *Streptopelia decaocto.*
Length: 11 inches.
Habitat: Suburban parks and gardens, and villages, especially near farmyards and chicken-runs.
Breeding Season: March to December, but mainly April to August.
Protection: Throughout the year, but may have to be deprived of protection if it goes on increasing.
Further Reading: See under *Birds* on p. 95.

BLACK REDSTART

Family: Thrush Family, Turdidae.
Scientific Name: *Phoenicurus ochrurus.* Common Redstart, *P. phoenicurus.*
Males are Cocks, *Females* Hens.
Length: 5½ inches.
Habitat: Open rubbly or rocky ground, often by the sea; nests in holes in walls or on ledges.
Breeding Season: April to July.
Protection: Throughout the year, with special penalties.
Further Reading: See under *Birds* on p. 95.

81

6

Bluethroat : Red-breasted Flycatcher : Yellow-browed Warbler

All three of the birds on this plate are passage migrants in small numbers on the east coast of Great Britain, more frequent in autumn than in spring, and most often seen along the east coast of England between Northumberland and Suffolk, and on two Scottish islands, Fair Isle between Orkney and Shetland, and the Isle of May in the Firth of Forth. While all of them are scarce, none is rare enough to figure in the annual reports on rare birds in Great Britain, which appear in *British Birds*.

The BLUETHROAT is a relative of the robin which, as its name suggests, is distinguished from other robin-like birds by a blue patch on its chin, throat and upper breast. This distinctive feature is, however, only found in the cock. Hen and young bluethroats are brown, somewhat resembling a robin without a red breast, although just occasionally the hen has a little blue on the throat.

Two forms of bluethroat visit us, one with a red spot on the middle of its blue throat, and the other with a white spot. The red-spotted form is much the more frequent, and visits us on its way to and from its breeding grounds in Scandinavia. The white-spotted bluethroat, on the other hand, breeds just across the North Sea in Belgium, Holland, Germany and Denmark. In their breeding territories bluethroats are rather skulking birds of marshy areas and watersides, but in Britain they are most often seen in coastal districts.

Like the bluethroat, the RED-BREASTED FLYCATCHER has never bred in the British Isles, but does so just across the North Sea in Denmark, which represents the tip of a wedge in a breeding range stretching away eastwards through Germany and the Baltic shores to Finland and eastern Europe. The red-breasted flycatcher is a tiny bird, no bigger than a blue tit, and looks like a spotted flycatcher with a prominent white patch on either side of the base of the tail. Cocks also have a red robin-like breast. Flycatchers are always easily told by their habit of flying repeatedly from a perch to catch insects on the wing, and the red-breasted makes identification easier by frequently flicking its tail to show the white patches at the base.

The YELLOW-BROWED WARBLER is our third smallest bird, being larger only than the goldcrest and firecrest (p. 84). It is one of the yellowish-green warblers known as leaf warblers, and looks like a tiny willow warbler or chiffchaff (both also leaf warblers), but it can be readily distinguished by its pale eyestripe and double wing-bar. Unlike the bluethroat and the red-breasted flycatcher, the yellow-browed warbler breeds as far away as northern Siberia, which makes it all the more surprising that it should appear so regularly on migration in the British Isles. It seems certain that these wanderers must be lost birds, for their normal wintering grounds are in southern Asia, from China and India south to Malaya.

ALL THREE

Males are Cocks, *Females* Hens.
Habitat: Most often seen near the
coast.
Breeding Season: Has never bred in
Britain.
Protection: Throughout the year.
Further Reading: See under *Birds*
on p. 95.

BLUETHROAT

Family: Thrush Family, Turdidae.
Scientific Name: *Luscinia svecica.*
Red-spotted Bluethroat, *L. s. sveci-
ca.* White-spotted Bluethroat, *L. s.
cyanecula.*
Length: $5\frac{1}{2}$ inches.

RED-BREASTED
FLYCATCHER

Family: Flycatcher Family, Musci-
capidae.
Scientific Name: *Muscicapa parva.*
Length: $4\frac{1}{2}$ inches.

YELLOW-BROWED
WARBLER

Family: Warbler Family, Sylviidae.
Scientific Name: *Phylloscopus in-
ornatus.*
Length: 4 inches.

Goldcrest : Firecrest : Dartford Warbler

Before the severe winter of 1962–3 the GOLDCREST was a fairly frequent, if never really common breeding bird throughout most of the British Isles. In autumn and winter, when great numbers immigrated across the North Sea each year, it was common in many parts of the south, often accompanying the winter flocks of tits. Since 1963, however, the number of breeding pairs has greatly decreased in most parts of the country, though it could not, except quite locally, be described as rare. Certainly the breeding stocks of goldcrests have been slower to recover from the effects of that disastrous winter than many other birds, such as the song thrush and wren. Nor have their winter numbers regained anything like their former strength, at any rate by the time of writing in the spring of 1966.

The goldcrest has the distinction of being the smallest British bird, at any time of the year. Its crest is orange in the cock, yellow in the hen. It is especially associated with coniferous trees, such as pine, spruce or yew, and almost always builds its tiny nest in one of them, usually slung on an outer branch well out of reach of man and other predators.

The FIRECREST is only marginally larger than the goldcrest, from which it can be told by its black-and-white eyestripes; both sexes have an orange crest. Its tiny size and double wing-bar further separate it from the otherwise somewhat similar leaf warblers, such as the chiffchaff and willow warbler, the great majority of which should anyway be out of the country by the time our few firecrests visit us each year. For the firecrest is a rare bird, except in the southern counties of England, where a few are seen in most winters. It has occasionally been suspected of breeding, but so far there is no published proof of this.

At the end of the hard winter of 1962–3, which so decimated the goldcrest, there can be little doubt that the DARTFORD WARBLER, our only resident warbler, was the rarest British breeding song-bird. Always a very local bird, confined to the heathlands south of the Thames, and long extinct at Dartford in Kent, where it was first discovered in 1773, the Dartford warbler had already been exterminated in Surrey during the hard weather early in 1962. Various estimates put the number of pairs surviving in the New Forest in the spring of 1963 at from four to seven, with only singletons in three localities in Dorset and 'a marginal remnant' in Devon. From that low point the Dartford warbler has been gallantly recovering, but it will be some years before it can hope to regain even its 1962 position, when there were still sixty pairs in the New Forest. It seems a far cry now to the pre-war years when a pair nested as close to Charing Cross as Wimbledon Common. To be sure of seeing one nowadays, it is best to go to the Channel Isles.

The Dartford warbler is a shy bird, rarely seen in full view except in spring, when it dances up in the air to utter its scratchy little whitethroat-like song. It is almost exclusively confined to heaths where the heather has been allowed to grow tall, though it also frequents dense thickets of gorse or furze.

84

GOLDCREST AND FIRECREST

Family: Kinglet Family, Regulidae.
Males are Cocks, *Females* Hens.
Length: 3½ inches.
Protection: Throughout the year.
Further Reading: See under *Birds* on p. 95.

GOLDCREST

Scientific Name: *Regulus regulus.*
Habitat: Woods, plantations, parks and large gardens, especially near coniferous trees.
Breeding Season: April to June.

FIRECREST

Scientific Name: *Regulus ignicapillus*
Habitat: Heaths, commons and scrub.
Breeding Season: Never proved to breed in Britain.

DARTFORD WARBLER

Family: Warbler Family, Sylviidae.
Scientific Name: *Sylvia undata.*
Males are Cocks, *Females* Hens.
Length: 5 inches.
Habitat: Heaths with long heather and thick gorse.
Breeding Season: April to June.
Protection: Throughout the year, with special penalties.
Further Reading: See under *Birds* on p. 95.

85

Summary of Rare and Introduced Species

Of the seventy-eight animals illustrated in this book, fourteen are mammals, fifty-two birds, six fishes and six butterflies. Altogether twenty-six of these are introduced aliens, the rest being either rarities, or at least scarce or local species.

Ten out of the fourteen mammals fall into the introduced group, namely, five species of deer, mink, rabbit, grey squirrel, coypu and edible dormouse. The remaining four (wild cat, pine marten, polecat and dormouse) are rare, scarce or local.

A number of introduced mammals have not been mentioned in the main text:

HOUSE MOUSE (*Mus musculus*): the longest established of all our introduced mammals, which probably arrived in the baggage of our neolithic ancestors several thousand years ago.

BLACK RAT (*Rattus rattus*): the plague carrier, which was probably responsible for the Black Death, and which is reputed to have come to Britain in the baggage of returning Crusaders in the twelfth or thirteenth centuries; today it is confined to certain ports and parts of Inner London.

BROWN RAT (*Rattus norvegicus*): our principal modern rat pest, which supplanted the miscalled 'old English' black rat during the eighteenth century.

WILD GOAT (*Capra hircus*): feral goats descended from medieval and later herds are widespread in the hills of Scotland, Wales and northern England.

A number of other introduced mammals are highly localized, such as the POLECAT-FERRETS (*Mustela furo*) on Mull, and the BENNETT'S WALLABIES (*Macropus rufogrisea*) on the moors on the Staffordshire–Derbyshire borders.

Several other mammals might also legitimately be included among the rarities:

SCILLY SHREW (*Crocidura suaveolens*): confined to the Scilly Isles.

ORKNEY VOLE (*Microtus arvalis*): confined to the Orkney Islands where, however, it is common enough to form the staple diet of the short-eared owl (p. 46) and the hen-harrier.

Four species of BAT: BECHSTEIN'S *Myotis bechsteini*, LEISLER'S *Nyctalus leisleri*, and the two species recently discovered in Dorset, the MOUSE-EARED *Myotis myotis* and the GREY LONG-EARED *Plecotus austriacus*.

Eleven of the fifty-two birds illustrated are introduced aliens, namely, five species of pheasant, red-legged partridge, little owl and four waterfowl: the Canada goose, South African shelduck and that handsome pair the Carolina and mandarin ducks. To these could be added such widespread and common species as the FERAL PIGEON (*Columbia livia*) of our towns, and the MUTE SWAN (*Cygnus olor*) of our lakes, ponds and rivers, together with several such more localized species:

BOBWHITE QUAIL (*Colinus virginianus*): from North America, now becoming frequent in parts of East Anglia as a result of deliberate introductions for sporting purposes.

RUDDY DUCK (*Oxyura jamaicensis*): also from North America, which has escaped from collections of ornamental waterfowl in various parts of the country and is currently establishing itself as a breeding species on a few reservoirs in the Midlands and the West Country.

EGYPTIAN GOOSE (*Alopochen aegyptiacus*): has a long-established breeding colony at Holkham Park in North Norfolk.

A score of the remaining forty-one birds are scarce or rare, but breed regularly in some part of the British Isles. Half a dozen of these are more or less confined to the Scottish Highlands, namely, golden eagle, osprey, ptarmigan, goosander, snow bunting and crossbill. A good many more could be added to this list, among them:

CRESTED TIT (*Parus cristatus*): confined to the pinewoods of Strathspey and neighbouring straths.

HEN-HARRIER (*Circus cyaneus*): regular in Orkney and becoming more widespread on moors further south.

DOTTEREL (*Eudromias morinellus*): a small plover that breeds only on a few of the highest mountain tops.

WHIMBREL (*Numenius phaeopus*): a familiar passage migrant on all coasts, but breeding only in Shetland, though it has occasionally done so on the mainland.

RED-NECKED PHALAROPE (*Phalaropus lobatus*): a dainty little wader that breeds in widely scattered localities on a great arc between Shetland and Co. Mayo in Ireland.

FORK-TAILED PETREL (*Oceanodroma leucorrhoa*): breeding only on the remotest islands of the Atlantic fringe of Scotland.

Three waterfowl: COMMON SCOTER (*Melanitta nigra*): a common winter visitor off the south and east coasts of England, which also breeds in Northern Ireland; and the two Grebes, SLAVONIAN (*Podiceps auritus*) and BLACK-NECKED (*P. nigricollis*).

Perhaps, too, one should now count as rare Highland breeding birds the REDWING (*Turdus musicus*) and both the WOOD and GREEN SANDPIPERS (*Tringa glareola* and *T. ochropus*), which now breed in most years in some part of the Highlands.

88

The two skuas, the GREAT SKUA (*Catharacta skua*) and the ARCTIC SKUA (*Stercorarius parasiticus*), which not long ago would have ranked as rarities, are now, thanks to protection, sufficiently numerous and spreading southwards from their far northern fastnesses to count as rare no longer.

Another seven of the rare breeders are mainly southern in their distribution, namely, hobby, bittern, avocet, yellow wagtail, Dartford warbler, black redstart and bearded tit. Of these the yellow wagtail is not in any sense a rare bird, except in Scotland and Ireland, but there are several other candidates for the title:

MARSH HARRIER (*Circus aeruginosus*): a fine bird of prey which, like the bittern (p. 60) was lost as a breeding species during the last century but returned under protection in the present one; it is still very rare, breeding in fewer than half a dozen extensive marshy tracts.

MONTAGU'S HARRIER (*Circus pygargus*): always very thinly distributed, but preferring the heathlands of the south.

BLACK-TAILED GODWIT (*Limosa limosa*): like the marsh harrier a bird which has regained its lost status as a breeding bird in a closely guarded site 'somewhere in England'; it has also nested in Scotland more than once in the past thirty years or so.

LITTLE RINGED PLOVER (*Charadrius dubius*): one of our newer colonists, which has come in since 1938; upwards of 150 pairs now nest each year, and it is only a matter of time before it ceases to be a rare bird.

WRYNECK (*Jynx torquilla*): has been steadily going downhill for a good many years, so that no more than twenty to thirty pairs still breed and these almost all in Surrey, Sussex or Kent.

MARSH WARBLER (*Acrocephalus palustris*): an elusive species, largely confined to the valley of the lower Severn and its tributaries.

There are also three species of which one can never be certain that they are actually breeding within the British Isles in any given year: HONEY BUZZARD (*Pernis apivorus*), GOSHAWK (*Accipiter gentilis*) and KENTISH PLOVER (*Charadrius alexandrinus*).

Two more of the rare breeders, the chough and the roseate tern, can be regarded as primarily western in distribution, and to these should be added the KITE (*Milvus milvus*), now restricted to Central Wales, although in Tudor times it was a common scavenger in the streets of London.

Finally we are left with a handful of more generally distributed breeding species which are not strictly rare at all, the collared dove and the goldcrest, which were rare when the plates were painted but are now steadily increasing; the little tern, which is decreasing and may before long actually be rare; and the short-eared owl, which is much more frequent in some seasons than others. Unfortunately, to these we now have to add both the PEREGRINE FALCON (*Falco peregrinus*) and the SPARROWHAWK (*Accipiter nisus*), which have reached a very low ebb as a result of excessive quantities of pesticide residues in their prey, though in the case of the sparrowhawk, which has only recently been protected, persecution by game preservers has also been an important factor.

Of the remaining twenty-two birds illustrated, six are winter visitors, the goldeneye and smew regular in some numbers, the firecrest regular in small numbers, and the waxwing, snowy owl and snow goose irregular in greater or less numbers. Ten more are regular passage migrants, the black tern and ruff in some numbers, but the rest (spoonbill, hoopoe, golden oriole, bluethroat, red-breasted flycatcher, yellow-browed warbler, and blue-headed and grey-headed wagtails) only in small numbers. The remainder are irregular visitors, mostly between spring and autumn, but appearing almost every year—bee-eater, roller, serin, gull-billed tern and rosy pastor. There are many other birds in each of these categories, far too many to be even listed here.

Only one of the six fishes illustrated, the char, is a native, the remainder (rainbow trout, common and crucian carps, ide and golden orfe) being introduced aliens. Other alien fish that would qualify for inclusion are the GOLDFISH (*Carassius auratus*), from Asia, naturalized in its greenish wild form in many ponds in suburban parks; the LARGE-MOUTHED BLACK BASS (*Micropterus salmoides*), from North America, established in several pools in the south; the BITTERLING (*Rhodeus amara*), from Europe, naturalized in at least eight localities in South Lancashire, their ancestors having been unwanted bait liberated by local anglers; and AMERICAN BROOK TROUT (*Salvelinus fontinalis*), naturalized in the Lake District and elsewhere.

Of the rarer native freshwater fishes not mentioned in the text, the most notable is perhaps the STURGEON (*Acipenser sturio*), a 'royal fish', any specimen of which caught in a British river belongs to the Crown. Then there are the various species of small salmonid fishes known as WHITEFISH (*Coregonus*)—not to be confused with the white fish of the sea, which are cod, haddock and so forth—and which resemble the char (p. 36) in their highly localized distribution in widely separated mountain lakes and lochs. They include the two VENDACES, *C. vandesius* of Lochmaben in Dumfriesshire and *C. gracilior* of Derwentwater and Bassenthwaite in Cumberland; the SCHELLY (*C. stigmaticus*) of Ullswater and two neighbouring lakes; the POWAN (*C. clupeoides*) of Loch Lomond; the GWYNIAD (*C. pennanti*) of Bala Lake in Merioneth; and the two POLLANS of Northern Ireland, *C. pollan* of Lough Neagh and *C. altior* of Lough Erne.

To complete the picture for British land and freshwater vertebrates, we should also mention the rare and introduced reptiles and amphibians. One each of our three native snakes and three native lizards are rare: the SMOOTH SNAKE (*Coronella austriaca*) and the SAND LIZARD (*Lacerta agilis*). Both inhabit the sandy heaths of southern England, where the snake feeds on the lizard, but the sand lizard also occurs on the dunes of the Lancashire coast. Our only introduced reptiles are a single colony of WALL LIZARDS (*Lacerta muralis*) in Surrey, and a possible breeding colony of the EUROPEAN POND TORTOISE (*Emys orbicularis*) in Suffolk.

The rarest of our native amphibians (three newts, two toads, one frog) is the NATTER-JACK TOAD (*Bufo calamita*), widespread but highly localized, liking marshy tracts by the sea. There are, however, two introduced species of frog, the EDIBLE FROG (*Rana esculenta*), whose status is very hard to estimate because frog enthusiasts are always releasing them in local ponds, especially around London; and the MARSH FROG (*Rana ridibunda*), which is locally common on and near Romney Marsh in Kent.

Of the six butterflies depicted, five are rare natives (two breeding and three migrants) and one, the large copper, is introduced. No other introduced alien butterfly has successfully established itself in Britain, although not for want of trying on the part of keen lepidopterists. The two rare breeding species are the purple emperor and the swallow-tail. To these, besides several others which are local rather than rare, might be added two FRITILLARIES, the GLANVILLE (*Melitaea cinxia*) and the HEATH (*M. athalia*); two HAIRSTREAKS, the BLACK (*Strymonidia pruni*) and the BROWN (*Thecla betulae*); two SKIPPERS, the LULWORTH (*Thymelicus acteon*) and the CHEQUERED (*Carterocephalus palaemon*); the much decreased and indeed now very rare LARGE TORTOISESHELL (*Nymphalis polychloros*); the LARGE BLUE (*Maculinea arion*), whose ant-loving caterpillar gives it the most extraordinary life history of any British butterfly; and the recently rediscovered BLACK-VEINED WHITE (*Aporia crataegi*).

The three illustrated rare immigrants are the monarch, the Bath white and the long-tailed blue. They might well be joined by the magnificent CAMBERWELL BEAUTY (*Nymphalis antiopa*), which may travel across the North Sea in Scandinavian timber boats; the QUEEN OF SPAIN FRITILLARY (*Argynnis lathonia*); the recently discovered BERGER'S CLOUDED YELLOW (*Colias calida*); and the now very rarely seen MAZARINE BLUE (*Cyaniris semiargus*), which probably did at one time breed in a few localities.

Some Wildlife Collections
and Nature Reserves

Obviously it is inadvisable to give away exact localities where rare animals and birds can be seen, but the following list includes a somewhat arbitrary selection of collections of wildfowl and other wildlife, and of nature reserves which are open to the public, as well as a few reserves where permits are required.

AILSA CRAIG, FIRTH OF CLYDE: well-known gannetry and colony of other sea-birds, easily seen from passing ships.

BASS ROCK, FIRTH OF FORTH: a similar sea-bird rock on the opposite side of Scotland.

BLAKENEY POINT, NORTH NORFOLK (National Trust): sand dune and shingle reserve, with terneries to which access is restricted in the breeding season.

BRISTOL ZOO, CLIFTON (Bristol, Clifton and West of England Zoological Society).

CAIRNGORMS NATIONAL NATURE RESERVE, INVERNESS-SHIRE (Nature Conservancy): reindeer, golden eagles, ptarmigan and other Highland specialities.

CHESTER ZOO (North of England Zoological Society).

DUDLEY ZOO, WORCESTERSHIRE (Dudley Zoological Society).

EDINBURGH ZOO, MURRAYFIELD (Royal Zoological Society of Scotland).

ELLESMERE, SHROPSHIRE: the Mere here, and neighbouring ones, are an important breeding station for the Canada goose.

EPPING FOREST, ESSEX (City of London Corporation): old-established herd of fallow deer, also nightingales, hawfinches and other woodland birds.

FARNE ISLANDS, NORTHUMBERLAND (National Trust): famous colony of eider ducks, and many breeding sea-birds, including terns.

HANDA, SUTHERLAND (Royal Society for the Protection of Birds): famous sea-bird colony on north-west coast of Scotland.

HICKLING BROAD, EAST NORFOLK (North Naturalists' Trust and Nature Conservancy): bitterns, bearded tits, and other Broadland birds (sailing unrestricted, but permits needed to land).

JERSEY ZOOLOGICAL PARK, LES AUGRES MANOR, JERSEY, CHANNEL ISLES (Jersey Wildlife Preservation Trust).

LOCH GARTEN BIRD SANCTUARY, STRATHSPEY, INVERNESS-SHIRE (Royal Society for the Protection of Birds): ospreys.

MINSMERE, WESTLETON, SUFFOLK (Royal Society for the Protection of Birds): famous marshland reserve on Suffolk coast, with bitterns, bearded tits, harriers, and now avocets (permit required).

HAVERGATE ISLAND, ORFORD, SUFFOLK (Royal Society for Protection of Birds): avocets, terns (permit required).

NORFOLK WILDLIFE PARK, GREAT WITCHINGHAM, NORWICH: includes collections of Ornamental Pheasant Trust.

NOSS, SHETLAND (Royal Society for the Protection of Birds, and Nature Conservancy): famous sea-bird island.

PAIGNTON ZOOLOGICAL AND BOTANICAL GARDENS, SOUTH DEVON (Herbert Whitley Trust).

PEAKIRK WATERFOWL GARDENS, NEAR PETERBOROUGH, NORTHAMPTONSHIRE (Wildfowl Trust).

RICHMOND PARK, SURREY (a Royal Park): famous herds of red and fallow deer.

SCOLT HEAD ISLAND, NORTH NORFOLK (Norfolk Naturalists Trust and Nature Conservancy): sand dune and shingle reserve, with terneries, to which access is restricted in breeding season.

SKOMER ISLAND, PEMBROKESHIRE (West Wales Naturalists' Trust and Nature Conservancy): Manx shearwaters and other sea-birds; grey seals.

SLIMBRIDGE WILDFOWL COLLECTION, GLOUCESTERSHIRE (Wildfowl Trust): the most comprehensive collection of ducks, geese and swans in the world, on the Severn estuary.

STANSTED WILDLIFE RESERVE, NORTH ESSEX; there is another wildlife collection not far away at Mole Hall, Widdington.

TWYCROSS ZOO PARK, ATHERSTONE, WARWICKSHIRE.

WHIPSNADE ZOOLOGICAL PARK, DUNSTABLE, BEDFORDSHIRE (Zoological Society of London).

WICKEN FEN CAMBRIDGESHIRE (National Trust): famous relic of East Anglian fenland, scene of attempts to reintroduce swallowtail butterfly.

WINDSOR GREAT PARK, BERKSHIRE (a Royal Park): mandarin ducks breed on Virginia Water and other lakes in the park.

WOBURN PARK, BEDFORDSHIRE: best collection of deer in Britain.

Some Useful Addresses

BOTANICAL SOCIETY OF THE BRITISH ISLES, c/o Department of Botany, British Museum (Natural History), Cromwell Road, London, S.W.7.

British Birds, 61 Watling Street, London, E.C.4.

BRITISH HERPETOLOGICAL SOCIETY, c/o Zoological Society of London, Regent's Park, London, N.W.1.

BRITISH ICHTHYOLOGICAL SOCIETY, 10 Whittliemuir Avenue, Muirend, Glasgow, S.4, Scotland.

BRITISH ORNITHOLOGISTS' UNION, c/o Bird Room, British Museum (Natural History), Cromwell Road, London, S.W.7.

BRITISH TRUST FOR ENTOMOLOGY, 41 Queens Gate, London, S.W.7.

BRITISH TRUST FOR ORNITHOLOGY, Beech Grove, Tring, Herts.

COUNCIL FOR NATURE, c/o Zoological Society of London, Regent's Park, London, N.W.1.

COUNTY NATURALISTS' TRUSTS COMMITTEE, Pyewipes, Willoughby, Alford, Lincs.

FAUNA PRESERVATION SOCIETY, c/o Zoological Society of London, Regent's Park, London, N.W.1.

FIELD STUDIES COUNCIL, 9 Devereux Court, London, W.C.2.

INTERNATIONAL COUNCIL FOR BIRD PRESERVATION, British Section, c/o Bird Room, British Museum (Natural History), Cromwell Road, London, S.W.7.

LINNEAN SOCIETY OF LONDON, Burlington House, Piccadilly, London, W.1.

MAMMAL SOCIETY, c/o Institute of Biology, 41 Queens Gate, London, S.W.7.

The Naturalist, Yorkshire Naturalists' Union, The University, Leeds, 2.

NATURE CONSERVANCY, 19 Belgrave Square, London, S.W.1; 12 Hope Terrace, Edinburgh 9, Scotland; Penrhos Road, Bangor, Caern., N. Wales.

ROYAL ENTOMOLOGICAL SOCIETY, 41 Queens Gate, London, S.W.7.

ROYAL SOCIETY FOR THE PROTECTION OF BIRDS, The Lodge, Sandy, Beds.

SCOTTISH ORNITHOLOGISTS' CLUB, 21 Regent Terrace, Edinburgh 7, Scotland.

SOCIETY FOR THE PROMOTION OF NATURE RESERVES, c/o British Museum (Natural History), Cromwell Road, London, S.W.7.

WILDFOWL TRUST, Slimbridge, Gloucestershire.

WORLD WILDLIFE FUND, British National Appeal, 2 Caxton Street, London, S.W.1.

Further Reading

GENERAL

The Ark in Our Midst, by R. S. R. Fitter, Collins, 1959.
Wildlife in Britain, by Richard Fitter, Penguin, 1963

MAMMALS

British Mammals, by L. Harrison Matthews. New Naturalist, Collins, 1952.
Field Guide to British Deer, by F. J. Taylor Page, Mammal Society, 1959.
 The Handbook of British Mammals, edited by H. N.Southern, Blackwell Scientific
   Publications, 1964.
Mammals in Britain, by Michael Blackmore, Collins, 1948.

BIRDS

The Birds of the British Isles, by David Armitage Bannerman, Oliver & Boyd, 1953–63;
   12 vols.
The Handbook of British Birds, by H. F. Witherby and others, Witherby, 1938–41;
   5 vols.
Pocket Guide to British Birds, by R. S. R. Fitter, Collins, 1952.
The Popular Handbook of Rarer British Birds, by P. A. D. Hollom, Witherby, 1960.
The Return of the Osprey, by Philip Brown and George Waterston, Collins, 1962.
The Waterfowl of the World, by Jean Delacour, illustrated by Peter Scott, Country
   Life, 1954–64; 4 vols.

FISHES

The Fishes of the British Isles, by J. Travis Jenkins, Warne, 1936.
The Freshwater Fishes of the British Isles, by C. Tate Regan, Methuen, 1911.

BUTTERFLIES

Butterflies, by E. B. Ford; New Naturalist, Collins, 1945.
The Butterflies of the British Isles, by Richard South, Warne, 1921.
Looking at Butterflies, by L. Hugh Newman, Collins, 1959.